Tricky Teens

How to create a great relationship
with your teen ... without going crazy!

Andrew Fuller

FINCH PUBLISHING
SYDNEY

Tricky Teens: How to create a great relationship with your teen… without going crazy!

First published in 2014 in Australia and New Zealand by Finch Publishing Pty Limited, ABN 49 057 285 248, Suite 2207, 4 Daydream Street, Warriewood, NSW, 2102, Australia.

14   8 7 6 5 4

There is a National Library of Australia Cataloguing-in-Publication entry available at the National Library.

Edited by Emend Editing
Editorial assistance by Megan English
Illustrated by Fiona Katauskas
Text typeset by Meg Dunworth
Cover design by Ingrid Kwong
Printed by McPhersons Printing

Finch titles can be viewed and purchased at **www.finch.com.au**

Contents

Section Three: How to change things at home   198

Section Four: Essential conversations to have with your teens   260

Acknowledgements

Author notes

Pledge to my teenager

Dear Teen,

I am your parent. I am *not* your friend, pal, bestie, mate or BFF. I repeat, I am your parent.

This means there are times that I will use the word 'No'.

This means what it sounds like. You will not like it when I use this word.

Toughen up and get over it. There will be times that you will think you hate me. There will be times that you think I am the worst parent on earth. There may be times that you are right even though you won't hear me admit it.

As a parent I am responsible for raising you to be a decent successful human being who treats themselves and others with tolerance and respect.

That is my job and I take it on willingly because I love you and want the best for you. This means that I will watch you with a level of surveillance that most intelligence agencies would envy. I will track you like a bloodhound. I will detect illicit or mind-altering substances with the intensity of a customs officer. I will scrutinise your love interests. I will check whether you have schoolwork to do and whether you are doing it to the best of your ability.

I will speak to your teachers without asking your permission. In fact, I will talk to whomsoever I please without your agreement.

I will call the parents of your friends at times, especially when there are parties.

In the house that I work to pay for, there will be rules. You will not like all of these rules. These rules are in place so I do not go crazy while raising you.

You have the right to argue with me. You do not have the right to remain silent or brush me off with vague comments like 'don't know', 'as if' or 'that is so random'.

I'm sure we are going to get along just fine. Through all this, please know that I love you for who you are and will continue to do so even if you screw up.

Love,

Your parent

For all the tricky teens …

Introduction

Teenagers are, essentially, mad.

Whether you call it 'not enough sheep in the top paddock' or 'all the pigeons aren't fluttering in the loft' or 'the lift doesn't always arrive at the top floor', there are times during the adolescent years when teens aren't the sharpest tools in the shed.

Don't get me wrong. I also think they are wonderful, but sheeeesh, they have their moments. The sooner you face this, the better. Realise that you are handling a privacy obsessed, hormonally erratic, mood-swinging, temperamentally unstable, planning-deficient creature on an emotional roller coaster and you have made the first step towards saving your sanity.

Of course, successful parenting is about love, warmth and positive regard. It is also about swashbuckling, feigning, acting and swaying the crowd. It'd be enough to make your average pirate pale and run in the other direction.

This book is about doing less with more. It is a compilation of ideas that I have collected, nicked, purloined and borrowed over the years. It is the secret knowledge of survival in a business that buries its martyrs.

As one mother described it, 'After years of being a helicopter parent, my rotors finally stopped whirring and I crashed to the ground. I looked at my children and said to myself, "You're all old enough to make your own mistakes, it's up to you now," and if I'm honest, I should have done it years before.' 'Black-hawk-down parenting' was her term for it.

The art of raising tricky teens and remaining sane is curiously elusive in today's embattled world. I hope this book gives you some nifty tricks to have up your sleeve.

Signs you might be stuck

Do you ever feel like you are going over the same old ground and getting nowhere fast? ☐

Are you arguing with your teenager about the same issue over and over again? ☐

Are you leaving for work in the morning feeling dejected and agitated? ☐

Are you coming home dawdling and taking the scenic route rather than facing the inevitable evening battles? ☐

Are you a single parent juggling roles, schedules, demands and requests but coping with none of them completely? ☐

Are you a step-parent who feels like every time you try to parent, your new partner and their teen gangs up against you? ☐

Your teen complains to you that you love their younger brother or sister more than them and you secretly think they might be right? ☐

You offer to take your teen on a holiday with the private, never-to-be-spoken-out-loud wish that they will say, 'No I'd prefer to stay at a friend's place.' ☐

Do you sometimes wonder whether the old Chinese proverb that you either marry or give birth to your worst enemy from a past life is actually true in your case? ☐

Whether your family is traditionally nuclear, single parent, step-blended or even tribal, these issues apply to you. If any of these ring true for you, you are caught in a grindingly exhausting dance that lurches through painful old routines. This book is designed to help you to change the patterns and create a new dance with your tricky teen.

Resilient parenting

It is highly likely that your tricky teen will survive your parenting. The really important question is, 'Will your lovely personality and temperament remain in place throughout the journey?'

There may be moments when you feel like you are a hostage. You may feel like your life has been kidnapped by a dramatist with erratic mood swings, unpredictable demands and a temper that would match Genghis Khan on one of his more tetchy days. Of course you love them. Of course you want the best for them. Of course you want them to be happy. None of this means you have to sacrifice your life to become a quivering shadow of your former self.

The question is not whether your teen will grow up and thrive, that's the easy bit. The big question is, will you survive their upbringing with your sanity, looks and good humour intact.

Here are a few life-preserving pointers to begin with.

Be a thief!

Steal, borrow, pinch and pilfer ideas and strategies from other parents. Give credit where credit is due but steal all the same. People have great ideas. Use them. Don't ever be accused of re-inventing the wheel. Good parents borrow books and ideas, great parents use them to create changes. This book is based on the guerilla tactics used by thousands of parents.

Rituals

One of the strongest predictors of good mental health is the presence of positive rituals in people's lives. The small regular things that we do to keep our lives sane don't have to cost much, and they don't have to take up much time, but they make a huge difference.

Have some rituals in your life each week that bring you and your family together. It doesn't matter whether it's the Friday night pizza or the Wednesday evening swim or the Sunday movie. Putting them in your diary at the start of the year and sticking to them is what matters.

Ask your teen for help

This is really hard to do. Often, it seems far easier to just do it yourself than to explain how something should be done. Teens can be a valuable time-saving resource, but only if you take the time to train them and ask them. People can only feel involved if you give them something to be involved in.

Parenting is an impossible job

Recognise it! Face facts. No one can be on top of everything all the time. Even the best parent, on their best day, under ideal conditions, is only going to be switched on about 20 per cent of the time.

Some tricky teens have a powerful investment in announcing that you are the worst parent on earth and that no one else's parents are anywhere near as bad as you are. Most parents of teens will confess that there are times when it doesn't matter what they did, it was wrong in the eyes of their teenager.

Generally, parents enjoy raising a family but look back and think, 'Phew, we all got through that relatively unscathed.' Parenting is the biggest, the best and at times, the toughest job going. For most parents, raising one family is enough. Perhaps this is why we see so many smiling grandparents with a twinkle in their eyes. Knowing that parenting is an impossible job may help you to throw away the guilt.

It's only an emergency if you have to call a crisis line

There is a growing trend to treat everything as if it is important, essential and an emergency. This leads some people to run their family in the same manner as they would run a psychiatric crisis clinic. We're there to raise children. What is urgent is not always what is most important.

Taking a 'steady as she goes' long-term perspective on things is important. This is especially true with tricky teens. When an issue arises ask yourself, 'Will this matter twelve months from now?' If the answer truly is 'Yes', do something about it. At other times it may be better to do nothing at all.

Grab an advisor

Some parents I know have a few people they regularly share the dilemmas of parenting with and chat with on a reasonably regular basis throughout the year. In some cases, these people are also known as drinking buddies. While soaking yourself in alcohol won't solve the issues, adding a support team will. Parenting is so complex that no one person has all the answers.

Give up 'busy' and 'not bad'

The busy world we live in leads people to sink into a quagmire of brief, dull interactions. For example:

'How are you?'   'All right' or 'OK' or 'Not bad.'

'What did you do on the weekend?'   'Nothing.'

'What did you learn at school today?'   'Nothing.'

Tricky teens are often the masters of the non-committal understatement – shrugging, mumbling and evading. Parents can counteract this by talking their world up and being positive.

Even worse is the discussion where everyone agrees they are busy. 'How are you?' 'Busy.' You've been busy too. We are all busy. You have as much time as everyone else. One hundred and sixty-eight hours every week. The same as everyone else. Pretend that it's enough. Don't fall into the self-fulfilling trap of saying to yourself and others, 'I'm too busy.' When you say, 'I'm busy' what you are really saying is ,'I am too busy for you.'

Keep a blue day book

There are days for all of us when we feel fed up. Having a book of good memories reminds us of the good moments and helps us get through the hard times.

Whenever something delightful happens, keep a record of it in your blue day book. If your children write you a card or give you a drawing, keep it in the book. For all of us there are moments when we feel our children don't appreciate us and it is really useful to be able to pick up those moments of good times and remind ourselves that it is all worth it.

Make a life calendar

Find an old calendar that you like. Don't buy a new one unless you have to. On the page that is the current month, put copies (or originals if you prefer) of good things that have happened in your family's history during that month. Hang the calendar in a prominent position in your house. The kitchen is often a good place. Then, as each month passes, make a small commitment to add good things that have happened in that month to the calendar.

By the end of twelve months you will have a calendar that represents and reminds you of the best of life. If your family is like every other family I have done this with, you will find there is one month when not much has happened. There will be one month that has been dull. Use this to inspire you to do something positive in that month.

Life calendar

Jumping January	Fantastic February	Marvellous March
Amazing April	Magnificent May	Joyous June
Jam-packed July	Awesome August	Sensational September
Outstanding October	Notable November	Dynamic December

Important things to know about your teen

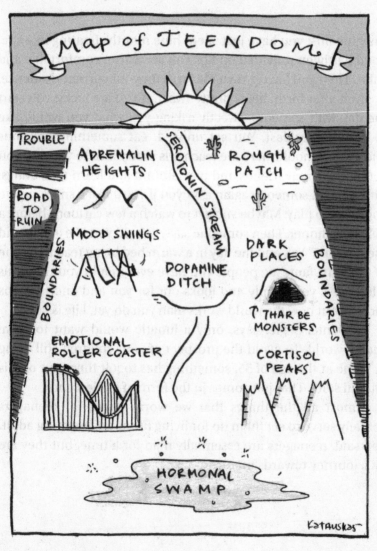

Welcome to the war of independence

Imagine this: you have just spent nine months floating in a spa. Food has been provided on tap. You are warm, comfortable and calm. Then you have grown too large for your current residence.

Even after birth, life is pretty sweet. If you are lucky, you start the day with someone sweetly asking you what you would like to eat for breakfast. You get dressed, eat something delicious and get to school where the teacher is pretty nice to you and you get to make new friends and play around and learn new things. After school, someone again asks you if you'd like a snack before going out to play. Maybe you get to watch a few cartoons before a delicious dinner. Then someone says, 'Would you like a bath and then a story?' You end the day in a warm bed being read to by one of the most fantastic people you have ever met in your life. This adult loves you deeply and looks out for you and knows heaps more about how the world works than you do yet. Life is good!

As Daniel Segiel says, only a lunatic would want to leave such a world. To avoid the prospect of your children still living at home at the age of 55, something has to jolt them out of this blissful state. That jolt comes in the form of adolescence.

Almost all the things that we worry about for teenagers actually serve to set them up for living life as an emerging adult. As I said, teenagers are essentially mad for a time, but they are on a journey towards maturity.

Common worry	Purpose for building adult skills
Can't organise	Need to learn systems for survival through experience
More distant from parents	Closer to peers – future relationships being developed
Intense interest in fashion and social media	Working out how to fit in with same age groups
Risk taking	Building peer acceptance
Thinking parents have no idea about anything	Focusing on new ideas and seeing how much they can be trusted
Shares ideas emotionally, dramatically and loudly	Testing their strength and power to change things

So, as your teen errupts out of the childhood years, it is helpful to know some of the pathways, jolts and obstacles you will face as they move towards becoming independent adults. While all tricky teens are unique and offer up some new challenges for their parents, there are predicable pathways through these years.

We are about to go on a roller coaster of parenting. It starts out gently and ends well, but along the way there are a few bumpy bits to contend with so grab your hat, take a firm grip, keep your head low and we should get through this relatively unscathed.

Teenage pathways

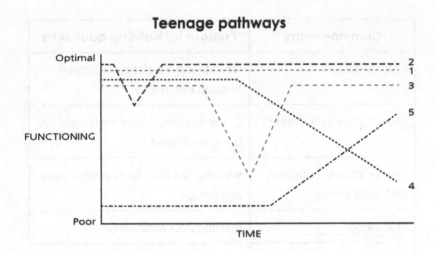

The pathway graph above will help you get some sense of your teen's behaviour over time. You may not always be able to neatly fit them into one pathway, but see if you can work out which one fits best.

Pathway 1 – Cruising through

Believe it or not, there are teenagers who cruise through these years. They mostly get on with their parents, they grumble, at rather than argue with their teachers and they do their homework pretty much on time. Since you have this book in your hands it is unlikely that you have one of these compliant, subservient, upstanding, commendable citizens in your home, at least not always.

Other parents always pretend to have one of these kids, which leads you to feel like a guilt-ridden abject failure in the parenting stakes. Never fear. When the lights are low and the door is closed, things may not always be as calm as they are portrayed. The grass is not always greener on the other side.

This is not to say that teens cannot be inspirational, funny, resourceful, ingenious and wonderful. Most teens are great, but it's also fair to say there are moments when their parents don't get to see the best of them. As part of the business of teenagers is to establish an identity separate from their parents', the best mix is to have a good relationship with some hopefully short-lasting, torrid differences of opinion.

Some arguments and some battles over independence are not a bad thing. There are some adults I see in therapy who never really managed to define their own identity, partly because they were so reluctant or too scared to ever argue with their parents. Teenagers should hold positions that are more idealistic and optimistic than their parents. As Philip Adams once sagely observed, 'Adolescence is a brief period of optimism separating a brief period of ignorance from a terminal period of cynicism.'

Pathway 2 – Hormonal hell

One of the first indications that you might be on this pathway is that your bathroom is no longer your own. A security barrier has been mounted around it and anyone approaching the zone is sent scurrying with screeches and squeals. Inside, the bathroom resembles a testing laboratory for a cosmetics firm. Lotions, potions, perfumes, hair straighteners or curlers accumulate. Steam billows and tempers reach flash point. Please note that I am not just talking about the girls here.

With almost half of eight-year-old girls now showing some signs of puberty, the world of tricky teens has got younger.

Add to this the delayed age of leaving home and you've got an expanding issue facing most parents.

The impact of hormones on early teenagers is enormous. For girls, estrogen hits the young female body like a freight train, making it more vulnerable to stress. It increases between ten and twenty times between 8 and 14 years of age. Up to about the age of twelve, it is boys who most often get diagnosed with psychological problems, from this age on, it is girls and women. Boys have a twenty-fold increase in testosterone around the same age. This means that if sex is ever off the agenda ... No, forget it! Sex is always on the agenda.

> Teenagers don't even recognise themselves.

The onset of puberty is a time of lowered functioning for many young people as hormones, body growth, increased irritability and mood swings can dominate their relationships. The impact of the changes in early adolescence is so extreme that teenagers don't even really recognise themselves. That is why if you turn to a thirteen-year-old and say, 'Do you remember when you were ten and we did ...', they will often respond by saying they don't remember. The extent of the changes they are undergoing makes their own life experiences foreign to them.

Pathway 3 – Mid-adolescent dip

This pathway is notorious. These teens strike terror into the hearts of their parents. For parents, these are the teens who cause furrowed brows, premature greying and sleepless nights. They make teachers think about retirement.

This group of teens fiercely displays their growing independence through risk-taking, getting out at night, associating with troubled young people, shoplifting, drug use and dangerous driving. They are looking for adventure or whatever comes their way. They can get into scrapes with the law, they may use drugs and alcohol, they may steal and they may have an ongoing, exhausting battle with their parents. Desperate parents feel that their teen is uncontrollable and on a highway to hell.

Parents may be tempted by television shows featuring brat camps, super tough judges and stern nannies threatening consequences or organisations that seem to want to break the spirit of these untamed teens. They can easily get the message that they have been too soft and are paying the consequences for being duped by their own child.

Parents can also receive a lot of unhelpful advice and grim predictions about the future of these teens. Other people will often predict that a teen in this group will end up on the streets or in jail or worse – dead from a fight or accident. The research indicates this is almost always not true. Despite the dire predictions made on behalf of these fiery teens, they mostly end up fine. The overwhelming majority pick up rapidly and function well.

> Parents can also receive a lot of unhelpful advice and grim predictions about the future of these teens.

Many of our finest adults had a bit of a rough period in their mid-teenage years. They inhaled a few substances, had a few scrapes with the law, got into a few brawls or into a few beds they would have thought more cautiously about had their frontal lobes been fully functioning at the time.

Parents often receive a lot of unhelpful advice from people who think they are wiser:

'Throw them out of the house.'

'They need tough love.'

'Let them experience the real-life consequences of their actions.'

If you follow this advice, I will tell you what happens. They get worse. Much, much worse.

Stick with these kids. You may not be able to control them. You may feel you have absolutely no positive influence in their lives for a time. All you may be able to do for a time is to support them, love them, stand by them and keep them alive.

Pathway 4 – Adolescent decline

This is a puzzling group of tricky teens. They have often spent their childhood and early teen years functioning well. They usually come from caring, loving families. Then, often around 16 years of age, they slump. Some spend longer and longer in their bedrooms. Others become part-time attenders at school. Some use illicit drugs. Others socialise with a small, similarly troubled group of young people. Almost all of them become hostile and uncooperative with their parents. Usually, the level of antagonism and anger in the family home escalates to intolerable levels and the parents seek some form of help.

I have seen so many teens on this pathway, both girls and boys, that I want to describe where the pathway leads. When these teens come in, usually accompanied by fearful, timid parents who have had to bribe them to get them through my door, their first action is to tell me how bad their parents are. The teens relate a litany of injustices. They may say their parents love the other children more than them or they are harshly restrictive or too lax and uncaring.

When you have worked as a therapist with as many tricky teens as I have, you take these claims with a grain of salt. Nevertheless, I listen to them as they recount the unfairness of life and their battles in response to this.

When I work with teens, it is a bit like fly-fishing. I often offer an idea and dangle it as bait in front of a tricky teen, only to whisk it away before they can reject it. With teens in this pathway, the first bit of bait I use is to say something like, 'Despite all of that, it seems that you are a good person.' Initially the teen may look warily at me so I may need to present this idea in several ways before it gains a sliver of acceptance. Once I have a sense that the teen is not going to totally reject my comments, I dangle my second piece of bait. 'Who else knows that you're a good person? I can't be the first who has seen this about you. I mean, I'm good, but I'm not that good.' If I pause and wait and give them time to respond they will often say, 'Grandma knew,' or 'Granddad knew,' or 'My sister knew,' or 'My Uncle knew.'

> When you lose someone as a child, you ... lose part of yourself.

At this point, I could take a fistful of money and place a large bet that the next thing that they will tell me is that Grandma, Granddad, sister or uncle is no longer available to them either through death or family dislocation. What becomes clear is that behind all that anger is grief. When adults grieve, they feel sad and tearful and mourn for lost people and missed opportunities. Teens don't do that. When teens grieve, they get angry. The loss of this person is not always recent. It may have occurred many years earlier. Sometimes it is a pet that is being grieved over.

When you lose someone as a child, you don't just lose the person. You also lose the part of yourself that was reflected in their eyes. These teens are heading into the future but are bringing with them an incomplete sense of themselves. They have lost whatever Grandma, Granddad, sister or uncle knew about them. They have spent a lot of energy covering up that loss with anger. To get beyond the anger, they need to re-acquaint themselves with the hidden part of themselves that Grandma, Granddad, sister or uncle knew.

This is how we all resolve our grief. We carry on our lives by incorporating the lost person's memory and aspirations for us, into our lives.

Pathway 5 – Adolescent turnaround or recovery

There is a group of teens who have had troubled childhoods and lives. The outlook for their future looks bleak. Despite this, many of them enter their late teens and early twenties functioning well. In the early 1990s, a research team consisting of Dr Karen McGraw, Melinda Goodyear and myself commenced a study that continues to this day on what it takes to turn young people like this around. Essentially, we have been studying the factors that allow teens to be resilient in the face of life's challenges.

In interviews and focus groups of this group of people, three factors emerged:

1 Being loved by your family Even in a really dysfunctional family, a teen who has one family member who loves them and thinks they are wonderful can be sufficient to turn that young person around from poor to positive functioning. This means that if the family setup is less than ideal and you can't overhaul it completely, just changing the way you and your teenager relate to each other will have a positive effect on their resilience and future life.

2 Having a diversity of friends   A teen doesn't have to be the most sociable, outgoing, gregarious or popular person about, but if they have a few choices in relation to friendship groups, this will protect them. Teens define themselves partly by the friends they hang out with. Having a variety of social groups avoids them getting locked into only one way of being.

3 Having positive connections outside the family   The third factor identified was the presence of a trustworthy adult outside the family who is able to form a positive bond with the teenager. This could be a teacher, therapist, sports coach, girl guides or scout leader, a church member or a neighbour who was able to form that positive connection. The young people we interviewed reflected that the positive adult was able to look beyond the smokescreen of their behaviour at that time.

A common sentiment was, 'They were able to see something in me that I couldn't see in myself.' The power of these adults to create a powerful turnaround in the young person's life is so impactful that I think that they gave the young person a gift that they will spend their lives unwrapping.

The active ingredients in developing resilience that will lead to a positive outcome for tricky teens are fairly straightforward: love them and think they are wonderful, make sure they have a range of friends and find another adult to believe in them.

These may seem fairly easy to achieve, but first we need to get around all the negative interactions that camouflage this from happening. If you want to keep informed about our research in this area, go to www.resilientyouth.org.au

Neurochemistry and habit

I don't want to begin by shocking you *too* much, but most tricky teen behaviour is not the product of conscious thought. It is highly unlikely that your tricky teen thinks to herself, 'My mother would be thrilled if I did that' or 'Dad would be chuffed if did that.' No. Most tricky teen behaviour is caused by two things:

1 Routines and habits; and

2 The neurochemicals and hormones washing around in that massive soup bowl called their brains.

Let's deal with the neurochemicals first. Emotions rather than reason rule the teen brain. Emotions are powerfully influenced by neurochemicals in the brain.

An essential thing to know about the teenage brain is that the emotional and security systems of the brain, known as the limbic system and the amygdala, are much more quickly activated than the frontal lobes. The frontal lobes are the part of the brain that says, 'Hang on a minute, this may not be such a good idea. Maybe we should plan something else.' Reflecting and re-considering are not strong features of the teen brain. In the heat of battle, these skills go missing entirely. Add an audience to the mix and these skills don't even bother showing up in order to go missing.

Parents are the people in the house with the frontal lobes that work. Parents are able to do something teens find difficult – planning, prediction and anticipation. This is why parents of teens need to turn to their kids at some stage and say, 'I'm the only one in the room with a fully functioning set of frontal lobes!'

A message to you, moody!

Tricky teens easily fall into moods and once they are in a mood it is hard to shift. This is why it is useful to know about creating moods.

When moods are intense, it makes other moods or states of being inaccessible. When you are parenting a tricky teen in an intense mood, whether it be anger, jealousy, sadness, hostility, happiness or worry, it is useful to know that the full repertoire of behaviours are not accessible to them.

They can't just pick another feeling off their mental shelf and feel that instead. That is why saying to someone who is feeling really worried, 'Just stop worrying,' doesn't help.

You can't change intense emotions until you change the brain's neurochemistry.

You may know this. If you have ever been *really* angry with someone, you might have noticed that you were unable to think of anything good that they had ever done. Later, on reflection, you are able to see a more balanced picture of the person. We are blinded by our moods.

Teens believe in their moods absolutely. This is why parents of tricky teens need to be skilled in creating moods, knowing how to change them and knowing when to walk away and battle another day.

Moodologist

Parents of tricky teens need to become experts in the art and craft of changing moods – moodologists if you like. You also need to be acutely aware that you can't change a teen's mood until you alter their neurochemical balance.

A tricky teen in a powerfully negative mood has about as much chance of seeing their parent's perspective and being convinced by it as a rampaging rhino has of delivering a bouquet of flowers.

The moods that teens experience aren't just to do with what's happening that day. It might come as a shock, but their moods aren't always your fault. Their moods aren't even understandable to them. Some of their moods have nothing whatsoever to do with you. They have to do with the chemicals running around in their brains and bodies.

When parents hear this, they often heave a sigh of relief. It explains why some behaviours come out of the blue, without warning.

There are a few key brain chemicals worth knowing about. This knowledge has the power to change your family.

Two brain chemicals parents of tricky teens would usually like to see less of are:

- Adrenaline
- Cortisol.

Two brain chemicals parents of tricky teens would usually like to see more of are:

- Dopamine
- Serotonin.

Our levels of these neurochemicals are changing all the time. Nevertheless, when we have large ebbs and flows, we often see predictable behaviours.

The Neurochemistry of tricky teens

Rate your tricky teen on the following issues then add a, b, c, d, and e together to get a total for each box (3 = very often, 2 = sometimes, 1 = occasionally, 0 = rarely).

Dopamine	Cortisol
a) Finds it difficult to focus on the task	a) Reluctant to ask questions when they don't know something
b) Doesn't feel motivated to achieve goals	b) Often can't state what they know
c) Is not proud of accomplishments	c) Is precious about their belongings
d) Seems lethargic and tired	d) Stresses a lot and worries about small things
e) Uninterested and won't have a go	e) Appears worried and watchful
Total Score	Total Score

Adrenaline	Serotonin
a) Is a real chatterbox	a) Seems shy and wants to disappear in social situations
b) Argues and disagrees too much	b) Is sullen and hard to talk to
c) Reluctant to try new things	d) Hard to please and doesn't like being praised
d) Does silly things	c) Hard to get going in the morning
e) Can be really busy without actually getting much done	e) Often says, 'Why do we have to do this?' and seems uninspired
Total Score ☐	Total Score ☐

As a rough guide, high scores (seven or above) indicate you should consider altering their neurochemical balance. A high score in dopamine or serotonin means that it is worth considering ways to increase the levels of these neurochemicals. A high score in cortisol and adrenaline means it is worth considering ways to decrease these neurochemicals. Let's look at these neurochemicals a bit more closely.

Adrenaline = revved up and snappy

You can tell when there is a lot of adrenaline around. Teens are chatty, ratty, scatty and highly distractible. They will talk over you. They may become motor mouths, making silly inappropriate comments. Before you've had a chance to respond, they're off on some tangent, leaving you scratching your head.

Adrenaline is partly responsible for the revved up, red-cordial high. It can make teens wired and snappy. Living on adrenaline energy causes teens to burn the candle at both ends with bursts of activity followed by long slumps of recovery. As many teens burn brightest late at night, this means midnight revelry followed by a slumberous morning.

Adrenaline makes teens less flexible and more rigid. It makes it harder for them to change their moods. When there is a lot of adrenaline, the amygdala or the fight–flight area of the brain is very active. This is the security part of the brain that works to defend you against threats or tells you to run away from them. This part of the brain can get so active that it takes over almost everything else.

You might know this yourself. Perhaps you've had a day where someone said something mean or nasty and you haven't felt your usual self for the rest of the day. That is at least partly because you were threatened and your adrenaline levels were raised.

Once a tricky teen gets an adrenaline rush, trying to change their behaviour is a waste of time until you've lessened the amount of adrenaline in their system. Signs that a tricky teen is having an adrenaline rush include demanding, driven behaviour or the 'I gotta have it now's', difficulty getting to sleep, lots of energy, silly 'hyper' behaviour, running off upset, door slamming or lots of conflict and disagreement.

Signs that a teen may have high levels of adrenaline

- Silly hyper behaviour

- Difficulty getting to sleep

- Lots of energy

- Storms off if upset

- Squabbling and bickering

- Restless and jumpy

- Reluctant to try new things

- Lots of busyness but not much gets done

- More talkative than usual

You can lower the levels of adrenaline in tricky teens by creating family routines and rituals. Rituals could include family dinners, walks, electronic-free times, movies or shows. These are times to catch up with one another. Regular family rituals promote belonging, safety and a sense of 'this is the way we do things'.

Rather than responding to their latest drama with operatic bouts of your own, develop a slow methodical manner with your teens. (We'll talk about applying this technique to arguments and develop a cooldown/meltdown strategy in the issues section.)

If your teen is prone to bouts of high adrenaline, develop clear, calm strategies. Know that we've been here before and we'll be here again. If you really must take a stand about something, restrict your comments to a few key points. If you try to negotiate on too many fronts, it will all blow up in your face. Adrenaline makes teenagers erratic, so too many issues to deal with causes them to flit from one issue to another, resolving none, and becoming more agitated and wildly dramatic in the process.

If your tricky teen is prone to the high wire antics of adrenaline, try to keep them away from energy drinks. Many of these drinks contain caffeine which sends levels of adrenaline skyrocketing.

> You can lower the levels of adrenaline in tricky teens by creating family routines and rituals.

Cortisol cowboys and cowgirls

Cortisol is the stress hormone and it gets released with adrenaline. If adrenaline makes your teen wired and snappy, cortisol makes them edgy and antsy. Being stressed and revved up can be a potent mix in households.

Pieter Rossouw describes cortisol as being like a delinquent roaming around seeing what trouble it can get itself into. Cortisol lowers language functioning. Have you have ever been so shocked that you couldn't put your thoughts into words? What happened then was that cortisol flooded into the language production centre of your brain (known as Broca's area), shutting it down temporarily.

Tricky teens who are under lots of stress often have great difficulty putting their thoughts into words. Cortisol also affects memory, which partly explains why teens under pressure often can't explain their actions or thought processes. It is also why stressed teenagers often reply in short phrases or monosyllabic grunts. School can be incredibly stressful for teens. For some it is a hostile jungle full of bullies, negative judgements and dangers. This can cause them to be on guard and self-conscious.

Like adrenaline, cortisol lessens teens' ability to change tack. It also reduces the ability to filter irrelevant information, which partly explains why people who are stressed can find it difficult to prioritise. Signs that tricky teens are cortisol cowboys or cowgirls include being worried and watchful, easily upset, on edge, easily tired, non-communicative, being unusually defensive and over-reacting.

Signs that a teen may have high levels of cortisol

- Difficulty expressing thoughts
- Worried and watchful
- Easily upset
- Nervy – prone to stomach upsets, headaches, odd unexplained pains
- Defensive
- Over-reacts to things
- Pessimistic – predicts negative outcomes
- Finds it difficult to prioritise

Parents of tricky teens can aim to decrease the amount of cortisol. As well as family routines and rituals, making teens feel safe from violence, ridicule or humiliation also decreases cortisol. Ensure teens do not have too much sugar and they drink enough water.

Getting enough sleep lowers both adrenaline and cortisol. Exercise is beneficial in re-setting teens' brains. As cortisol is closely related to feelings of anxiety, if your teen seems to have high cortisol levels, see Anxiety and worry busting on page 36. Fluorescent lighting has been associated with elevated levels of cortisol. Families with tricky teens would be better off with indirect lighting such lamps, especially in the evenings.

Dopamine = Pumped up and raring to go

Dopamine is the switched on, pumped-up neurochemical. It is good for feelings of pleasure and motivation and it's the party animal of the neurochemical world. Dopamine helps people change moods. It approaches adult levels somewhere between six and nine years, then lowers during the teenage years. This explains why teenagers can be harder to motivate than younger children. Dopamine also plays an important role in shifting and directing attention and concentration. There is evidence that some families may have patterns where they have more difficulty than others when shifting from focusing on one activity to another.

> Altering your behaviour to suit the circumstances is an important life skill.

Altering your behaviour to suit the circumstances is an important life skill. Flexibility is associated with mental health and resilience. You don't want to behave at a job interview the way you might at a sports game. How a teen behaves with their friends should be different than how they behave in class at school.

Signs that tricky teens may be low in dopamine include loss of motivation, being lethargic and tired, seeming disinterested and unwilling to have a go and not being proud of their achievements.

Parents of tricky teens may want to increase dopamine levels. Several things can help with this:

- Activities that involve repetitive movements such as table tennis, dancing, ice skating, juggling, skateboarding, surfing, swimming, down ball or handball and drumming.

- Solving challenges and problems – asking your teen to help you by working out a solution to some family issue.

- Social interaction – there is an increase in dopamine when teens mix socially with others.

- Use of rewards, inducements, bribery – call it what you will, it works!

- Dietary supplements of tyrosine and omega 3 and 6 have also been associated with increases in dopamine.

Signs that a teen may have low levels of dopamine

- Difficulty focusing
- Unmotivated
- Not proud of accomplishments
- Listless, lethargic and tired
- Uninterested and won't try things out
- Finds it unsettling or difficult to shift from one activity to another

Computer games are great builders of dopamine. So much so, once the game is completed, teens are usually depleted in dopamine and therefore, motivation. Trying to get a teenager to do anything after a prolonged period of playing computer games is a lost cause.

If this seems relevant for your teen, please read the issue on Computer addiction on page 92.

Serotonin – the quiet achiever

Serotonin is the most powerful antidepressant known to humankind.

Teenagers often have low levels of serotonin, which explains why they might see life as less pleasurable. They are prone to grumpiness. While dopamine gives you the pumped-up high, serotonin is the quiet achiever. It is the slow high and accompanies calm, considered decision-making.

> Serotonin is the most powerful antidepressant known to humankind.

Signs that tricky teens may be low on serotonin include being hard to please and unresponsive to praise, hard to get going in the morning and needing a reason to do things. They might ask 'Why do we have to?' or they're sullen and uncommunicative, avoiding eye contact and unwilling to participate in family activities. Low levels of serotonin are linked to depression.

Serotonin can be increased by exercise. Whereas activities with repetitive movements increase dopamine, exercise of any kind will raise levels of serotonin. Giving positive, warm feedback also increases serotonin as does giving tricky teens some choice, control and areas of responsibility.

Some tricky teens lead very pressured lives where they are required to fit into someone else's schedule. Some tricky teens, for example, experience their school days as a form of imprisonment – bells ring, they are marched from room to room at someone else's beck and call. No wonder they're grumpy. Ensure your teen has time at home when the pressure is off and they can do as they please. This freedom contributes to serotonin levels. Uninterrupted sleep is also a big serotonin builder. Too much caffeine and artificial sweeteners such as aspartame reduce serotonin. Try to keep tricky teens away from these.

Signs that a teen may have low levels of serotonin

- Grumpy, sullen and uncommunicative

- Harder than usual to get going in the morning

- Hard to please

- Doesn't respond to praise

- Everything seems to be a bother

- Sad or depressed

If there seems to be a prolonged pattern of low serotonin, a psychological assessment may be beneficial.

Parents of tricky teens can keep levels of serotonin high by following some of the guidelines in the section Ideal day (see page 134). They can also influence serotonin by providing lots of positive feedback, support, touch, love, humour, fun, exercise and opportunities for social interaction.

Habits and routines

Teens are creatures of habit. They do the same things in the same way over and over again. Habits are shortcuts for our lives. Rather than thinking things out from scratch, we follow the same sequences of behaviour. This is why couples and families argue about the same issues over and over again.

Teens are more habit-driven than most, simply because they have less capacity to plan. The result of having your frontal lobes partially closed for reconstruction is that you tend to do the same things in the same ways.

Charles Duhigg in his wonderful book, *The Power of Habit*, says the loop at the core of every habit is:

Cue → Routine → Reward

A cue sets off a change in the neurochemical balance that kickstarts a sequence of behaviours that result in a reward.

Let's go through a typical scenario. A parent comes home to find their teen lying on the couch playing computer games and says, 'Hi, how was your day?' The teen replies non-committally. After some time has elapsed, the parent re-enters the room and asks, 'Don't you have homework to do?'

This is the cue that launches the routine. A tirade of disputes emerge about the relevance of school in today's society, the association between homework and child abuse, why educators incarcerate children and ruin the best years of their lives and how parents are stupid enough to join this conspiracy.

At a critical point in this routine, the parent becomes affronted and starts to refute the points alleged by the aggrieved party. At this point fireworks are added to the routine in the form of yelling, accusations of being a conformist agent of a dying society rebounded by despairing comments about the homework avoider's future if key school assignments remain uncompleted. This escalates to slamming of doors, feelings of being misunderstood and a return of the teen to his or her bedroom. The reward is that the homework remains undone.

This habit sequence can create insanity in parents. It is not that it occurs that is the problem. It is that it occurs over and over again in a mindless repeating loop that is so close to hell you won't know the difference.

> The habit sequence can create insanity in parents.

Before outlining a six-week process designed to help you improve the way you and your tricky teen interact, I have included a series of common issues that range from anxiety to raising twentysomethings. Hopefully not all of these issues are relevant for you. You could either read the issues that you feel relate to your situation or continue along to Section three.

Helping teens overcome common issues

Anxiety and worry busting

Anxiety is contagious. If one person gets it, it can spread to the whole family. There is no shortage of things for teens to worry about: body size, popularity, school marks, appearance, romance, sex, friendships, talents and the future are just some common concerns.

Teens are more vulnerable to worries than adults and less capable of thinking their way out of them. It often falls to the parents of teens to hose down the worries, settle their minds and help them to return to doing things fairly productively.

Anxiety robs you of happiness. It prevents the serene experience of being in the moment and enjoying it. Just when the sun is shining and the flowers are in bloom and you could be sniffing the breeze and considering whistling or humming a tune, anxiety rushes you off to some future event that you probably can't control or to some past wrongdoing that you suddenly feel you should worry about or feel ashamed of.

> Anxiety robs you of happiness.

Given the amount of rushing about people do, you could be excused for believing that the general level of anxiety is on the rise. You'd be right. Stress levels have been steadily climbing over the past few decades and the people who feel it most are teens. The hormonal roller coaster of adolescence means they feel grumpier and are more affected by the slings and arrows of existence.

As well as robbing teens of happiness, anxiety also makes them reluctant to try new things. They keep doing the same old things in the same old ways. Life becomes pretty dull if you are stressed out, overly cautious or a perfectionist (see Perfectionism on page 148).

Parents of tricky teens who are anxious need to know how to lessen stress. Teens are often so wrapped up in their own world they don't pause to question the validity of their thoughts or feelings. This is part of the parents' role as moodologists.

There are three ways of dealing with anxiety:

1   Distract it.

2   Dissect and analyse it.

3   Be aware of it and let it be.

Distract

There are effective and ineffective ways of soothing anxiety. We could put distraction into the 'ineffective' basket except for the fact that so many people use it. Look around and you will see people buying alcohol, placing bets, arguing about small details or pretending to be something they are not, all in an attempt to disguise the fact that they feel anxious.

People have this strange idea that it is a dreadful thing if other people know that they are feeling anxious.

> *Teen rule for anxiety: Everyone feels anxious but no-one is allowed to show that they feel anxious.*

Feel the terror of a teen at a social dance eyeing off potential friends and partners while trying to look as cool as a penguin. Relate to the teen who after a poor day at school, throws a hissy fit and gets into a horrendous argument with a parent over an unrelated issue.

Distraction leads to tricky behaviours. By trying to conceal our anxiety, we behave in ways that threaten our closeness to others. Of course the things that we use to distract ourselves from anxiety can become problems in themselves and they never permanently address the concern. Anyone who has gone on a holiday after a stressful period knows that distraction works … for a time.

Things teens can do to lessen anxiety	What teens *actually* do to lessen anxiety
Decrease caffeine, nicotine, sugar, alcohol and drug consumption	Sleep less
Give up energy drinks	Argue with parents
Eat a diet low in sugar and saturated fats	Use social media
Breathe from the diaphragm	Talk to friends
Practise mindfulness	Play computer games
Relaxation techniques	Play sport
Exercise – even a 10-minute walk helps relieve anxiety	Dance
Stretching, yoga, tai chi	Listen to music
Slow down the pace of living, plan less for your day and plan to have some down time	Eat junk food
Sleep – get to bed at 10 pm and wake no later than 7 am	Drink energy drinks

Stop catastrophising	Write poetry, songs
Learn that a feeling is just a feeling and it can't hurt you	Do nothing
Plan what to do if you do start to panic	Get grumpy
Get some counselling to regain perspective	Blame others
Replace negative thoughts with positive ones	Find someone who has the same worry and consider them to be an expert in the area
Live a balanced life – put the system back into the chaos of life	Complain about unrelated matters
Get organised	Stop doing schoolwork
Creative arts therapy	Yawn, act tired and tell people how stressed you are
Hypnotherapy	Use drugs
Meditation – focus and relax the mind	Become a couch potato
Spirituality	Drink alcohol
Creative play	Become disruptive at school
Go out into the sunshine – vitamin D relieves anxiety	Go over and over the same old worry

If you pause to think about it, you might ask why most people do such stupid things to avoid feeling anxious. We drink, gamble, argue, fight, escape, avoid important deadlines, put off important tasks, procrastinate or become controlling in a usually ineffective attempt to stop feeling anxious.

To simplify things a bit, think of your brain as being in two parts. The first is the brilliant, insightful, creative and compassionate brain that evolved most recently in humans. It's still going through a few refinements and has a few wonky patches especially in the teen years, but as a work in progress, it's doing pretty well. Oliver Emberton cleverly describes these parts of your brain as Albert and Rex. Let's call your genius brain Albert.

The second part of your brain evolved a long, long time ago and forms the bottom part of your brain. We could talk about the reticular activating system and the basal ganglia but it is more fun to call this part of the brain Rex.

Rex is very old, can get quite grumpy and isn't very bright. Rex doesn't use language. He doesn't use logic much either, so he can't be reasoned with. Also he is incredibly easy to distract.

Now we all like to think that Albert runs the show. We are all reasonable, intelligent people in control of our own destinies, right? Wrong! Rex runs the show. At times Rex will listen to

Albert, but only if it is something Rex wants to hear. For example Albert might decide to go on a diet, but if Rex wants to lie on the couch watching soap operas and eating chocolate fudge, I wouldn't jump on those scales for a while. If Albert says, 'This issue isn't worth worrying about' but Rex detects a threat, you're likely to be up pacing the floorboards at 4 am.

Rex runs on neurochemicals and habits, not on words and reasoning. Comfort matters a lot to Rex. You can get Albert to take matters into hand but only if you distract Rex with something to keep him comfortable. Food, drink, sleep and rest all help Rex to settle for a while.

The problem for many of us, and especially teens, is that as soon as Rex is feeling warm and snuggly, we think the problem is solved and don't put Albert to work in sorting out the issue. Instead we take a break. Things are fine, we think. Until disgruntled Rex roars back to life. Then we start feeling anxious and fearful again.

Mental wellbeing is a lot like a rubbish bin. You can put the lid on really, really tight and try to make sure the smell doesn't get out but if this doesn't work, you might have to open up the bin and find some way of cleaning it out. If you can't keep the lid on and distraction is not working to reduce anxiety, you need to move to a more analytical level. You need to put Albert to work.

Dissect and analyse

Rather than wasting time ruminating over worries, fix them. The approach of dissecting and analysing stress arises from the idea that anxiety is an over-reaction. By getting things into perspective, you will feel less stress. While teens generally have more Rex than their parents, none of us are entirely free of anxiety.

Anxiety is the reason you are here. We are all the descendants of cautious, paranoid pessimists. Your ancestors weren't the people who said, 'Ah, it looks a bit like a sabre-toothed tiger but it will be fine.' Those casual laid-back types were the ones who got eaten. The wary, wired types survived. Your ancestors survived by being cautious and watchful. They paid attention to their worries. Considering whether the rustling in the leaves could be an animal that wanted to attack them allowed them to survive and produce you!

> Those casual laid-back types were the ones who got eaten.

So now you know. It is all your ancestors' fault. In fact, anxiety is everybody's ancestors' fault and dooming and glooming is usually an over-investment in a tiddly, temporary problem. It's not surprising, then, that at times your brain wants to send you danger signals to protect you even when there isn't any danger.

The strategies outlined here apply to both teens and their parents. Everyone gets anxious. There is no shortage of things to worry about. All people worry at times. It is part of being human. Do I look OK? Am I popular? Will I be successful? Can I do this? What will people think of me? In fact, if we're not careful, we can waste a lot of our lives worrying about things that never happen. The following strategies are designed to help you worry less – or at least only worry about the things worth worrying about.

Albert Strategy 1: Write out your worries   Our anxieties ricochet around in our head, causing us to go over and over the same old thoughts. Getting your worries out of your head and written down on a piece of paper is a good start to managing anxiety.

Albert Strategy 2: What is the worst thing that could happen? Look over your list of worries and analyse them. When we worry, we think something dreadful is going to happen. Bring the fear out into the light. Write down a few sentences about what you fear will happen if the thing you are worrying about comes to pass. And then write a few more sentences beginning with, 'And then I will ...' This won't always lessen your worries but it will make it clear to you what the consequences are and tease out some possible outcomes.

Albert Strategy 3: Worries are shifty   Now, rate your worries as to how permanent they are likely to be. It's highly likely that the things you are anxious about now are not the same as the things you worried about a year ago. For your teen, this is especially true. This is also likely to happen to your current worries, so it can be a useful question to ask yourself, 'Is it likely that I will still be worrying about this one year from now?'

Albert Strategy 4: Evaluate your investment   Now take your list of worries and place a value on each one. Give your worry a money value of up to $100. For example, having a family member leave might be a $100 worry, failing at school might be $70, getting an answer wrong in a test might be a $30 worry. Now estimate a money value for the amount of time you are spending worrying about a problem. If you're spending $5 of worry on a $100 problem, you might need to think about what more you could do to solve the problem. If you are spending $100 of worry on a $5 problem, you might want to consider if you are overdoing it.

Albert Strategy 5: Your brain believes what you tell it   Our brain is intelligent, but it is also stupid. While your brain can keep you up at night debating the pros and cons of the minutest concern, it is also powerfully influenced by what you do and what you tell it. If you act calm and confident, the Rex part of your brain often falls for the trick and releases serotonin to calm you. If you drink some water and do some exercise, not only does the stress hormone cortisol metabolise and lessen, you also feel better.

Your posture also has an effect. If you stand up straight and assume a powerful posture, your body tricks your mind into

believing you are confident. Cortisol decreases and testosterone increases when you hold yourself in a powerful posture such as both hands raised in a victory stance or a wonder woman position with hands on hips and one hip thrust forward.

For a great video on the power of posture, have a look at Jane McGonigal's TED talk on the game that can give you ten extra years of life.

Getting to know your teen's Rex: warrior or worrier

Before we all label ourselves as stressed-out drama queens, we need to acknowledge there may be a genetic side to all of this. This might seem a bit technical, but it's worth it.

A Taiwanese study compared students who were taking a stressful school test that determined their future. The researchers were interested in the COMT gene. This gene carries the code for an enzyme that clears dopamine out of the Albert part of your brain, aka the pre-frontal cortex. It seems we can be roughly divided into people who have one of two variants of this gene. One variant slowly removes dopamine and the other rapidly clears it. Let's call the group with the slow-clearing gene the 'drippers' and the group with the fast clearing variant the 'gushers'.

The gushers can be thought of as warriors who are ready for action at a moment's notice. They are up and at 'em. Meanwhile, the slow-clearing drippers are more contemplative, philosophical types who thoughtfully plan while scratching their chin. They solve problems slowly.

> In many schools, speed is king. The first to finish... wins the day.

In many schools, speed is king. The first to finish, come up with an answer or complete a timed assessment wins the day. Gushers often get the accolades in school, leaving their more hesitant dripper friends in the dust. Of course, in human history we have relied on people who are fast acting *and* people who think slowly and methodically to flexibly create solutions to problems.

As discussed in chapter 2, dopamine is the neurochemical that is responsible for creating motivation. Under usual circumstances, the drippers, the people with the slow-acting gene, do better when solving problems. They concentrate longer, solve problems more clearly and have higher intelligence. Slowly, slowly does eventually catch the fishy. But under stressful conditions like a nationwide test for entrance into schools or a high impact school day, it is the rapid-draining gushers who do better.

Most of us are probably a bit of a mix of dripper and gusher, although there are people we can all think of who are furiously headstrong or painfully hesitant. The question for us – and for teens – is how do we bring the best of our potential qualities to the fore?

A study conducted by Jeremy Jamieson at the University of Rochester using undergraduate students gives an answer. Students were given a statement about the effects of stress on performance. Half were also told that, 'people who feel anxious during a test might actually do better … therefore … you shouldn't feel concerned … simply remind yourself that your arousal could be helping you do well.' Just reading this statement significantly improved performance. The students who were told to see anxiety as helping their performance scored 65 points higher than the others. How we view anxiety powerfully determines our physical response.

> Most of us are probably a bit of a mix of dripper and gusher …

In another study of women working in motels changing bedding, one group was told this must be an exhausting and stressful job and were warned to keep a look out for their wellbeing. The other group was told that this is a wonderful job as you get a physical workout while doing your job. The group who were told about the health benefits of their job scored much healthier on measures on follow up. The way we view things is powerful. Nothing new there.

If analysing anxiety, writing it down, realising it is all your ancestors' fault, assigning values to worries or telling yourself stress improves performance hasn't helped, what else can you do?

Be aware of it and let it be

Our third main way of dealing with anxiety is based on the contemplative eastern meditative traditions. Being aware of our feelings and accepting that they are there and that they will pass is a skill most teens only learn when someone teaches it to them. Perhaps you know some of these feelings?

- Dizziness and vertigo
- Being drenched in sweat
- Embarrassment
- Shortness of breath
- Trembling and buckling knees
- Shaking hands
- Flushed face
- Racing heart

No-one likes these feelings. The problem is, the more you try to control them, the less controllable they become. If you've ever tried to feel less embarrassed, you know it is impossible. The more you focus on these feelings, the stronger they become. Your system is revving on cortisol and adrenaline. It has perceived a threat and wants to mobilise to keep you safe from that threat. Working against a system that is trying to save your life is futile. Instead, you can try to accept the **stream** of life:

Stop.

Think about and notice the feelings you are having.

Recall that that you have had feelings like these in the past.

Every feeling passes, even the anxious ones. It is just a feeling. You've had feelings you haven't liked in the past and you've survived.

Accept that these feelings will be there until they pass.

Move. Your body is trying to rev you up so give it something active to do and enable yourself to shift your focus.

Anxiety takes time to dissolve. When teens confront a new situation, they often want to avoid it. Parents who encourage their teens to keep having a go and to not worry about the result help them to broaden their worlds. When we focus too much on the outcome of something rather than the way of doing it, teens stress out, give up and become unmotivated.

Arguments

Healthy families have arguments. If there is no conflict, there is no growth. It is the *way* families argue rather than the arguing itself that makes the difference. Family dynamics are like a debating competition. One team wants things to change, the other team wants them to stay the same.

The 'change' team (usually the kids) say things like:	The 'stay the same' team (usually the parents) say:
I want to go out more	It's a school night
I need more pocket money	You know what your allowance is
I want to leave school	You need to finish your schooling
I'm going to a party	We need to call their parents
My girl- or boyfriend is staying over	You're not old enough
Everybody else is allowed to	Everyone else is not my responsibility
All the other parents let their kids ...	I don't care what other parents do

It is through debating these sorts of issues that families grow up and develop. While differences of opinion and disputes can be useful, they can also leave you gasping and exhausted.

Some ways to argue

It's better out than in   It is better to have a disagreement about an issue than to leave it smoldering away where it can go underground and form into resentment or sabotage. As long as everyone …

Fights fair   Arguments are often hot issues but rarely are they do or die (even if it seems so at the time). Argue to win by all means but keep an eye out for your long-term interests. Your relationship with your teen is more important than almost any issue so always keep an eye out for …

Seeking a solution   While not always possible, try to aim to reach a solution that is seen as fair, not one with a sense of coercion. Punishment does not change behaviour. It breeds resentment and secrecy. Even when there is a heated difference of opinion, seek a resolution that is seen as fair and reasonable (if not unanimous). Violence is never acceptable. Parents have the final say.

> Arguments are often hot issues but rarely are they do or die …

Ignore the sneering, the pouting, the flouting and the shouting
Arguing with a teenager is a bit like mud-wrestling a pig – you both end up dirty but only the pig is happy. Teens love drama, soap opera, horror, gore, action and intensity. If you want to give them this level of amateur dramatics in your home be my guest, but my clear advice is that you will be wasting your breath.

Arguments require a minimum of two people. Any less and you have a monologue, a rant or a soliloquy. Willing or unwilling, at least two people need to be present to play. Argumentative teens are like tinderboxes; the slightest flashpoint will lead to pyrotechnics. Don't add fireworks to the bonfire. Keep your voice calm and quiet. If you need time to steady your nerves, take a few breaths and settle yourself before responding.

As we've seen, the hormones in your teen's brain have become more powerful and are more active in the emotional parts of the brain (known as the limbic system) than they are in the planning and impulse control parts of the brain (known as the frontal lobes and the pre-frontal cortex). For many teens there is a battle going on inside their own heads between the emotional limbic system and the more rational frontal lobes. The emotions win hands down.

The second change is that teens become hyper-aware of their own emotions. They become obsessed with privacy, easily embarrassed and get swept up in their own feelings. They are not so tuned into other people's emotions. The emotion they read least well in other people is fear.

> Teens often can't see the negative impact that their words or acts have on others.

That tells us there are two things that are useless to say to tricky teens. The first is, 'What are you thinking?' because they often won't know. The second is to ask, 'Couldn't you see your younger brother or sister was scared?' or 'Couldn't you see I was frightened?' because the answer they will often give is 'No.' No is the truthful answer. Teens often can't see the negative impact that their words or acts have on others. To consider the impact our actions have on other people requires not just empathy, but reflective thinking. Teen brains aren't set up for reflective thinking. They are set up for quick decisive actions.

Creating a culture of cooperation in your family

No-one wants to be in a family that argues all the time. It's stressful and dispiriting. When you have a rampaging teen in the house, most parents feel that they have about as much control as they would in front of a charging, disgruntled hippopotamus. Cultures of cooperation are fostered when family members treat one another with respect and are prepared to help one another out and be civil to each other. Cultures of cooperation do not occur by accident. They occur when the people running the family create them.

Choose which hills to 'die on'

A culture of cooperation does not mean that you just give up parenting and let them do whatever they damn-well please (tempting as that might feel some days). Teens have more energy to put into most battles than adults do. This means that parents need to select their battlegrounds very carefully. Narrow the issues you are prepared dispute. If you have too many issues, you will become exhausted and most likely ineffective.

Choose three key values

Narrowing the battlegrounds requires you to think very clearly about what is the most important areas of discussion for you and your teen. In the last section of this book we talk about essential conversations to have with tricky teens (see page 261) but here, let's talk about contentious areas.

To guide you, select three of the following areas and give them a priority listing of one, two and three. Your teen may not agree with your selection.

School work	Religion
Safety	Non-violent interactions
Drugs and alcohol	Computer usage
Helping around the house	Swearing
Stealing	Sex and relationships
Appearance	Tidiness
Treatment of siblings	Gambling
Rudeness	Sleep time
Coming to meals	Money

Many parents would have liked a few additions to the list, such as being considerate, respectful and pleasant. While these are admirable aims, they are often secondary to the main battleground. Also, once the arguments lessen, those are values that you will model to your teen.

It's not surprising if parents also start arguing with each other as well as with their teen because conflict is contagious. Raising tricky teens can make adults feel unsupported or misunderstood by their partners. If this seems to be the case, each parent should select one issue to go to the wall on. The other parent should agree to let them do the frontline parenting in relation to that issue and not to contradict them. Agree that you will argue tooth and nail, over *only* three issues for the next six weeks. The same goes if you are a single parent or a step-parent.

Start a cunning plan

In a fair and reasonable world, teens would have a blinding flash of enlightenment, see the errors of their ways and start behaving more sociably, politely and respectfully. And if you believe that, leprechauns may appear at the bottom of your garden. No. If change is to occur, you will be the one to kick it off. Ask yourself:

- What do I want to see start happening?

- What is one thing that I am doing that I should stop doing?

- What is one thing I am not doing that I should start doing?

- What is one thing I am doing that I should do more often?

- What is the first sign that things are improving?

Give up coercion Trying to force a solution to this argument has not worked so far. Admit it. Give yourself some time off from trying to solve the issue. Creating a family culture of cooperation takes time. Trust needs to be rebuilt on both sides.

Some teens are so wary, hostile and intent on seeing malevolent intentions in their parents' actions that every gesture is viewed as meddling or controlling. In these circumstances, parents may need to walk away from the specific issue for a time to let matters cool down.

Hit–and–run parenting Family arguments often have a pattern of stand-and-deliver debating with rising levels of tension followed by angry words, slamming of doors, departing the scene or seething and muttering. Zipping past a reclining teen, making a fast-flying compliment and moving along is a good strategy at this time. Don't wait for a response. Don't wait for even a grunt. A moving target is harder to hit and even harder to argue with.

Model positive interactions If a family has argued for some time, it is likely that the standard of courtesy and consideration has declined. To lift the bar of interactions, model hyper-courtesy in your home. Be dignified and polite. If grubby patterns of arguments have been ingrained for a while, don't be surprised when you find the level of family interaction has reduced to a level that would even make a politician squirm. Whenever possible, don't return to gutter fighting. Instead say, 'I don't have to stay and put up with this. I'll talk to you when you are able to be polite.' Then move away.

> A moving target is harder to hit and even harder to argue with.

Have set procedures Think carefully about the planning outline you completed, especially the part about 'What I should stop doing'. Study your argumentative tricky teen carefully. Learn to differentiate 'cooldowns' from meltdowns.

Cooldowns These are heated disputes that become emotional to the point that further discussion is unlikely to be productive. To give yourself space to regain your cool, have a cooldown phase. Try to learn what helps your teen to cooldown. It could be being left alone, listening to music, playing a computer game and sometimes even a hug and a reassuring word.

Meltdowns This is where the fight–flight part of your teen's brain (called the amygdala), has hijacked the rest of the brain. Once the internal security system has kicked in, there is no point trying to press for a solution. They will act wildly, say the most horrendous things and behave erratically. If you continue to intervene they will go berserk. Your teen's levels of the stress hormones, adrenaline and cortisol, have soared. Until they have settled again, negotiating with them will place you in a very precarious position.

This is the stage where you pull up stumps, call an end to the innings, sleep on it and live to deal with it another day.

The power of belonging The reason arguments with so many teens are heated is because they are effectively trapped. They are desperate for peer acceptance and freedom from you so they can appear independent. And yet they know they are dependent on you and want to belong to their family. They are bonded to you, but struggle against these bonds – they are also scared that the bonds might break.

Let teens know they are loved.

This means that it is important for parents to use every opportunity they can to let teens know they are loved, wanted and are proud of them. It also means that despite saying hurtful things that would seem to indicate that they hate you and want to be as far away from you as possible, teens are fearful of being abandoned by parents.

Parents, never underestimate your power. Part of the reason your teen argues with you is that they know they can rely on you. You are safe. You love them. They can express their angst and alienation with you. It is not always pleasant. Remember that healthy families argue at times and through these debates they grow and develop.

Changing family arguments One set of parents was tired of their family squabbling and niggling in the same old way. 'About as predictable and as exciting as a washing machine cycle,' is how they described it. Over several weeks they embarked on a plan that would either see their children call the authorities to have them certified or change the family forever. Their plan was as simple as it was cunning. I have outlined it here for you.

1 Draw a plan of your house and place this on the refrigerator door.

2 For one week take note of every fight and make a note on the map on the fridge. If possible, be seen to be rubbing your chin and muttering, 'Ah, yes another one.'

3 Under no circumstances explain your actions to your teen.

4 Intervene in disputes as little as possible during this time.

5 After a week or so, note down your family's style of arguing. Some are 'free-floating fighting families' who argue down the hallway through the kitchen and out into the bathroom while others like to argue just in one room.

6 Continue marking down fights on the map but start following your arguing family members around with a sound recording device. Tell them you are doing a research project and ask them to speak more clearly into the recorder. (Your teenagers will hate this.)

7 Finally, announce that the family should have a fighting time and place and recommend that this be in front of the television when your teen's favourite show is on.

Arguments feel like they flare up out of the blue but for most families, arguing is very patterned and predictable. Most families argue over the same issues in the same way over and over again. Altering small elements in the pattern often results in major changes to arguments.

Move from rules to principles   Families with young children need to have clear rules and boundaries. Many rules are to keep kids safe, such as don't cross the road alone. As children become teenagers, the negotiation of rules becomes a more sensitive issue. Defiance by teens, combined with their delusional sense of immortality, makes rule-setting necessary. The trick is not to have too many rules, but to be crystal clear about the ones you do have.

As soon as you can, shift from enforcing rules to creating a culture of cooperation. Teens almost always want their parents' love and approval even if they at times they act as if they are seeking the reverse. Have high expectations for your teens and try to build a culture of cooperation within your family. Who is appreciated, appreciates. Having a sense of 'this is the way we do things here' instills habits and practices of interaction.

Consider the core values you have in your own life and those you would like to see in your teen. Live them. Don't allow yourself to stoop to the level of a squabbling teen. It doesn't solve the problem, but it will provide them with plenty of entertainment. Eventually, try to have teens follow the golden rule – treat other people as you would like to be treated.

Belonging and attachment

Our sense of belonging is the most powerful antidote we have to suicide, violence and ongoing drug abuse. Our sense of belonging is the underpinning of resilience. Early patterns of belonging, security and attachment echo throughout our lives and play a major role in how we manage relationships. There is no love without some fear of loss. There is no attachment without some rejection. Even the most attentive, perfect parent in the world cannot be there for every gurgle, whimper and cry their baby makes.

We all have to grapple with the feelings of insecurity that accompanies the movement from total dependency as a child to self-reliance and inter-dependence as we grow. The way we dealt with that separation between our parents and ourselves creates our sense of belonging. It shapes how your teen relates to others and it also determines the way you parent your teen.

In our dealings with others, we often repeat the way we were treated as children. It is rare to sit back from the rush of life and rectify our early problems with the love and security we received. Because most of us don't do this, we are often destined to repeat the past. We re-inflict the same old wounds on ourselves and the people we love. Many of our relationships are the same damn thing over and over again. After a time, our relationships begin to resemble each other. We search for happiness in new, loving relationships but are destined to repeat the past. Different person, same old battleground.

One of the most powerful ways we can help our children to have wonderful lives is to give them a secure sense of belonging. To do that, we need to think about our own relationship patterns and to be aware of them.

Developing a secure sense of belonging and attachment

About half of us won the lottery of life. We were lucky enough to have a parent, parents or caregivers who helped us to develop a secure sense of belonging. They did this in three main ways.

Firstly, they helped us to put words to that morass of stuff we call feelings. They would say things like, 'You seem happy today', or 'Are you feeling angry about that?' or, 'Are you upset that that happened?'

Secondly, they helped us to learn that not everyone feels the same way that we do. If I'm feeling upset or angry, it doesn't necessarily mean that everybody else is feeling angry and upset with me. Learning to differentiate our own feelings from other people's takes a while.

Thirdly, they helped us to learn how to calm ourselves down. Learning how to calm ourselves is something we learn best from a loving parent who soothes us. By being soothed when we are upset, we learn to do this eventually for ourselves.

> Security goes a long way towards creating a happy life.

A secure attachment involves learning that you are loved and gives you a basic introduction to emotional intelligence: knowing your own feelings, identifying and sensing feelings in other people and knowing how to calm yourself down when you are upset. Having that security goes a long way towards creating a happy life.

How our sense of belonging can get distorted

Ideally, all of us would feel a secure sense of belonging and be able to set up strong, positive relationships with other people. Life, however, is rarely ideal. Some people's early experiences were fraught by poverty, family tension, relationship breakups, illness, post-natal depression or just tough times. For others, infant illnesses or temperaments made it difficult to feel secure.

Below are some common types of belonging and attachment and how to handle teens who display signs of either.

Avoidant belonging and attachment About a quarter of us develop an avoidant form of belonging and attachment. We are wary and distrustful of intimacy and close relationships. We resolved the disappointment of not having a parent available all the time by learning not to rely too much on other people. During childhood, we may become fiercely self-reliant, burn up friendships and not let ourselves be comforted by others. In romantic relationships, the big question becomes, 'Can I rely on this person?' As adults, we may sabotage or avoid close relationships.

Insecure belonging and attachment About a fifth of us become characteristically insecure and clingy in our relationships. (Before you become too self-diagnostic, remember that all of us can have bad days in our relationships. It is when this becomes a pattern that we would start to analyse ourselves.) Insecure attachment leaves us prone to being pessimistic, clingy, jealous, dependent on others and with rock bottom self-esteem. The most common feeling is of being unworthy of love. Children who are insecure often feel mystified when people want to be their friends.

Insecure people are often incapable of calming their fears or soothing themselves and rely on others to help them deal with upsets. Adults in this group start romantic relationships anxiously and worry about whether they are worthy of the person they are with. This can lead to panic and feelings of being abandoned whenever there is distance or conflict in their romantic lives. Being in love is filled with anxiety, but being without love is seen as unbearable.

How insecurity or avoidance shows up in the teen years

The teen years are a time of defining ourselves as people who are separate from our parents. It is a time of partial de-attachment. Early relationship experiences that set up a secure, avoidant or insecure sense of belonging are amplified in these years. Recognising if your teen is in one of these categories will help you in your relationship with them.

Parents want their kids to be happy. A powerful part of a happy life are the positive friendships and relationships we form around us. Knowing that teens with attachment issues are likely to sabotage these relationships means that parents should think long and hard about ways to help their teens regain a sense of secure belonging. This requires intentional planning and also the realisation that not all of your children need you to parent in the same way. Realise that trust and security are regained slowly, bit by bit.

> Not all of your children need you to parent in the same way.

Parenting an avoidant teen back towards security

Teens who are avoidant find it hard to trust close friendships and intimate relationships. They avoid them or, without even being aware of it, sabotage them. As children, they weren't cuddly kids. They never seemed to seek out a hug or get much comfort when you gave them a hug or kiss. Usually, they found it hard to share feelings. They can be wary and distant in conversations. Given that teens aren't always the most conversational of creatures, this means they can be pretty hard to connect with.

If these teens have had some trauma in their lives, they can also be highly reactive. This means they can fly off the handle in a rage with the slightest provocation. For some, these traumatic experiences increase their wariness, vigilance and risk-taking behaviour. The big question for avoidant teens is, 'Can I rely on this person?' The default answer for an avoidant teen to this question is, 'No, I can only rely on myself.'

Parenting avoidant teens back towards security involves a series of long-haul strategies.

1. Be consistent and caring Raising tricky teens can require the patience of a saint. Parenting an avoidant tricky teen involves implacability. As much as they can infuriate you with dismissiveness, offhandedness and apparent disinterest, calm and steady parenting wins the day. At the slightest hint of conflict they flare up or close the shutters and you don't get to relate to them for weeks. Reduce your rules to the absolute minimum. Focus on building the relationship.

> Some teens need to hear that you love them more than others.

2. Be there for them – regardless of the situation Constancy is the name of the game. Avoidant teens have an 'approach and disappear' relationship style. Parents who stand strong and consistently by their teens demonstrate to them that they can be relied upon.

3. Nurture them Some teens need to hear that you love them more than others. For this reason, go on a saturation, love-bombing campaign. Don't expect to get much appreciation or expression of love in return. The interaction may be something like this:

Parent: 'Guess what?'

Teen: 'Yeah, I know. You love me. OK, I've heard it.'

Don't be dissuaded. Making sure they really know they are loved works.

4. Teach accurate interpretations of others   Avoidant people often imagine that others are hostile. They may pick out someone and decide that person doesn't like them or disapproves of them. This can lead them to feeling hurt and slighted when nothing was intended. Teaching avoidant teens to read faces well is helpful. It also helps to understand that not everyone's feelings or intentions can be read accurately.

5. Gradually increase physical intimacy   Avoidant teens are not the most responsive bunch when it comes to hugs and physical warmth. Don't let this deter you. Hands on shoulders, ruffling of hair and quick friendly touches on the shoulders or arms can help. Even if they shrug you off, look for the next opportunity to touch them as you move past them.

> Rituals are useful for every family.

6. Build positive rituals of connection   Rituals are useful for every family but for avoidant teens, they are indispensable. Avoidant teens go missing in action. Avoiding family dinners, gatherings, celebrations and social functions is their preferred position. They practise absenteeism.

Make at least one meal a week mandatory to eat with the family (more if you can). Have a couple of family functions that are essential to attend. (You may also want to read the section on Reclusive teens on page 163.)

7. Be a fierce friend   Fierce friendship is the best definition of good parenting I've ever come across. It comes from the Buddhist tradition. A fierce friend does three key things:

a) They treat their relationship with you as permanent. There is no way out. We are going to have to work this out.

b) They are your biggest supporter. They are undeniably on your side.

c) They will tell you when you are talking garbage.

8. Use positive language   Use words like 'great friend', 'love', 'hug' and 'close'. People who are avoidant turn down the dial on the amplifier of emotion. Their typical responses are:

How are you?	Not bad
What have you been doing?	Not much
What did you learn today at school?	Nothing
Who did you catch up with today?	No one
Did you enjoy that?	It was all right

These teens are not exactly candidates for hosting talk-back shows. It's enough to have most parents tearing their hair out in frustration. In parenting avoidant teens, it is OK to turn up the amplifier on your own emotions. Practising exuberance and using words that communicate intimacy and closeness help parents model to these teens that it is fine to display and express positive emotions.

> Fierce friendship is the best definition of good parenting.

Parenting an insecure teen back towards security

The big question for insecurely attached teens is, 'Am I worthy?' Many of them don't feel loveable or desirable. They have low self-esteem. This can leave them desperate for love and at risk of trying to form a relationship with anyone who appears interested. These teens are so keen to fit in that they can be led by others and influenced by peer pressure. Some will try to buy friendship by paying for things, or providing things to please people.

If they think they can't fit in or be desired, some become outlandish and provocative to get a reaction. Any reaction, even a negative one, is better than being neglected. Some can be so intense that when they do make a friend, they scare people away. Some insecure teens cling close to their parents and don't stray far from home. Others seek out the wildest group they can and will sacrifice almost anything to identify with them.

Parenting an insecure teen back towards security takes time and effort, but it is extremely worthwhile. A few strategies that work are outlined below.

1. Stick to your word – follow through   Sometimes insecure attachments can occur as a result of a child's anxious temperament. More often it occurs as a result of tumultuous, changeable and uncertain events when they were young.

These events are often beyond everyone's control and may include grief, post-natal depression, relationship pressures, job loss, poverty or illness. Whatever it was that caused this, it leaves a sense of uncertainty in the family. Nothing can be totally relied upon.

Young children often see events in their family's lives as a direct result of their own actions. So, in child-logic, the uncertain times are seen as being caused by the child not being loveable, not good enough or worthy enough. As these children grow into teens they often seem hesitant, uncertain and insecure. It can seem like a kindness for parents to use vague, inclusive language with them by saying things like, 'We'll see if we can,' 'We'll try to,' 'We'll fit it in if we can.'

Parents use this 'maybe' language because they are kind and it sounds reassuring and considerate. The problem is that it mirrors the teen's uncertainty and heightens their anxiety. This anxiety may be expressed as worrying, but it can also be displayed as behavioural issues. For this reason, with insecure teens we need to practise crystal clear parenting: If my mother says it's going to happen, it's going to happen. If my mother says it's not going to happen, it ain't going to happen.

> 'Maybe' language mirrors the teen's uncertainty ...

2. Value them for who they are, not what they achieve Some of these teens can be so, so sweet and so, so lovely. They will tell you three thousand times a day that they love you. Now it's nice to hear a bit of the love stuff from teens but often there is a desperate air about it. It's almost as if they are thinking, 'If I tell you that I love you three thousand times, then you'll tell me that you love me and then maybe, maybe, maybe I'll feel better about myself.' It can leave a parent breathless!

Make sure that your teens know that you love them regardless of how well they do. Otherwise these kids will start spinning cartwheels to gain your love. Most of us would feel mighty pleased if our teens were so intent on impressing us, but with insecure teens, it's more a case of, 'Look at me! Look at me! Don't you love me?'

3. Don't give too much space to their negativity   Not to put too fine a point on it, these teens can also be whingers and worriers. Complain? They can complain until the cows come home.

We all want to understand our kids, to share their concerns and to empathise with them but as we all know, if you wallow in your own negativity for too long, people get tired of you. When you catch teens wallowing in negative thinking, it can be hard to require them to express some positives too, but it's worthwhile work for a parent. Firmly shining a light on the things they are doing well will help them to shift their mood. For more on this, you might like to read the issue on Pessimism on page 156.

4. Be watchful for perfectionism   Insecure teens can become perfectionists. The underlying belief is, 'If I am absolutely perfect then people will love me.' For some, this will lead them to be high- and perhaps even over-achievers who are scared of taking risks. For others, it may mean that they will not try or take on activities that they might make mistakes in because to make a mistake is to lose the chance of being loved. If you feel this applies to your teen, read the issue on Perfectionism on page 152.

5. Check out doubts and move on   Insecure teens can be great brooders. They can ruminate and grind ideas and worries over and over in their minds. For this reason, parents may need to teach them to check out their doubts.

It is an act of bravery to go up to someone and ask, 'So you don't want to be my friend, is that right?' And yet, sometimes it is better to know even if the answer is not the one you wanted to hear. This is especially the case for some insecure teens who otherwise go over and over the same doubt in their minds. Helping insecure teens to ask direct questions such as, 'Have I done something that has upset you?' or 'Are you angry with me?' saves them a lot of angst and brooding.

With these teens, be particularly careful not to feed their fears. Your helpful suggestions about how to approach things differently can be misinterpreted and itself become a source of brooding and rumination.

Boy smarts

Whether they are boys or girls, tricky teens have a lot in common with one another. Nevertheless, there are some nuances and parenting strategies that seem to work better for boys than girls. For that reason, this book discusses communication strategies separately, as well having sections for boy and girl smarts.

Teenage boys are the masters of minimalism and the practitioners of just-in-time management. Asked to do almost any task, their immediate response is, 'Later.'

Walk the dog?	Not now.
Feed the goldfish?	Later, they're still swimming.

In school, if they are asked to write a 50-word essay, they will count the words. If they write 51 words, most will think they have overdone it. Boys need more time to answer questions and work out what they want to say.

The following methods are likely to work in parenting the majority of boys, but with less competitive, sensitive boys, it can be more helpful to focus on them attaining their personal bests.

Respect

Teenage boys are constantly checking to see if you respect them. They respond well to people who have expectations of them and respect them as capable of meeting those goals. As the TV character Ali G would say, 'Respect!'

This is why asking for their assistance is helpful. Women throughout the ages have asked strong young men to open lids for them, shift bits of furniture or fix something. Most of it has been completely unnecessary, but gee it made those young men feel a million dollars. If a teenage boy has a sense that you respect him, he will walk over coals for you.

Clear signals about who is in charge

Boys need boundaries. They need to know who is in charge at home. Successfully raising boys requires parents to become benevolent dictators. Consult a lot, seek their opinion and assistance but at the end of the day you, the parents, are in charge.

Use a physical signal when you want silence   Boys need more visual and physical signals than girls partly because they are less tuned in to facial cues. They are also more able to screen out white noise. (Parents requesting attention equals white noise!)

When you really need to get a teen boy's attention, use visual cues such as raising one hand, turning lights off and on, moving to a particular part of the room, or opening or shutting curtains. Never yell. If a parent starts yelling at a boy, they often find they have to yell louder and louder. The parent becomes hoarse and the boy appears to be deaf.

Fewer rules and fewer words   Have no more than three clear rules that you apply fairly and consistently. Base your family management on the idea that, 'I'm not going to let you do that to your brother because I wouldn't let him do it to you. That is the rule.'

Value them and they will be heroes

Boys are tuned into hierarchies. This means the predominant values of a family plays a powerful role in determining their actions. Have a couple of core values (compassion, generosity, being part of a team). Live by them and insist upon them. Help boys to learn that they can be heroes and victorious, but that winning doesn't mean someone else has to lose.

Use knowledge from computer games as an inspiration for learning

Boys' attraction to competition will override almost any disadvantage or loss of motivation. They generally love competitive games, especially when there is not an ultimate winner. If you've watched a boy place rubbish into a bin you will notice he doesn't just drop it in, he takes a shot. Boys love a challenge.

Computer game designers have cleverly used the principles of engagement to captivate boys:

- Make success challenging but attainable by breaking it down into stages.

- Making success more likely than failure.

- Give people the opportunity to try again.

- Try to create a safe zone where boys can try new activities in a setting where there are no consequences.

The most motivating games have players succeed about 80 per cent of the time initially before building up to 100 per cent and moving to the next level.

Use lots of movement

Parenting boys is like being a cross between a matador and a traffic cop. Keep on the move and mingle with the crowd. Boys see things best in motion. Use visuals and animations as often as you can. For this reason, movement and aiming to achieve a set target are powerful strategies with boys.

Boys need quiet times

In order to reflect and re-energise, boys need quiet times to think, read and at times quietly chat with others. Arrange your home so that there are quiet spots for thinking.

Know about anger

Anger and shame can take over boys and once boys are angry, it is harder for them to get over it. If they feel you are going to shame them in front of their friends, they will fight you tooth and nail. Most boys will do silly, self-defeating things rather than lose the respect of their friends. Deal with issues at a time of your choosing, not when the boy wants to deal with it. If you really have to pick a battle with a boy, wait until you are alone with him.

There are also decision-making differences between girls and boys when involved in dispute resolution. Girls are often more able to see the effect of their actions on other kids so asking, 'How do you think she felt?' type questions may pay off. In contrast, boys are less cued into other kids' emotions, so a more successful strategy may reinforce a rule such as, 'We don't do that in this family.'

A whiff of success

Most men and boys waste an incredible amount of time completing tasks that don't need to be done and avoiding tasks that don't need to be avoided. Help them to structure tasks and to improve on early attempts so that they gain mastery and success. Once a boy believes he can be successful, he'll almost always live up to it. If he also knows you think he is wonderful, capable and clever he will try his hardest to live up to that.

Bratology

The following features define the Common Brat:

1 *Inability to delay gratification* The Common Brat has not learned to wait, and cannot tolerate frustration. Typical behaviours include whining, tantrums, tears and dummy spits.

2 *Failure to persist in the face of difficulty* Consistent with very low frustration tolerance, the Common Brat will give up on any activity that requires effort and persistence. The behavioural response is as above.

3 *Failure to empathise or recognise the needs of others* The Common Brat is focused on satisfying the self, and tends to view others as a means of self-gratification. Can become extremely hostile and competitive when territory is encroached, particularly if required to take turns or share. Behavioural response as above.

4 *Requirement to win at all times* The Common Brat does not like to share attention with anyone. This includes competitive games. Catastrophic responses in the face of not winning are to be expected! Approach with caution.

5 *Sleeping habits* The Common Brat is essentially a nocturnal creature. Extreme cases can be as adverse to sunlight as a vampire.

6 *Diet and grazing habits* The Common Brat demands a very narrow range of foods. Shunning fruit and vegetables, the Brat runs on caffeinated energy drinks and copious amounts of junk food. Deep-fried potato and instant noodles are often sought when grazing. Foods that are coloured green are often avoided.

> The Common Brat is focussed on satisfying the self.

7 *It is all about moi!* The Common Brat does not reflect on the consequences of their actions. Consideration of others does not enter the question. If asked to take others' needs into account, the behavioural response is as above.

8 *Ideal habitat* The Common Brat prefers a climate with minimal expectations of competency and effort. A compliant adult is essential to maintain a constant level of satisfaction and to predict and pre-empt any potential frustration.

Displays of temper must be met with immediate attempts to soothe and appease. Above all, successful breeding of the Common Brat must avoid opportunities for learning emotional regulation and self-calming. The adult must avoid this by intervening whenever upsets occur. These may include disappointments and frustrations, or variations of plans.

The Common Brat must be carefully cultivated, and is of a different type altogether from other species which may share some characteristics. This arises from developmental difficulty. The Common Brat may manage to avoid maturity for many years, even into adulthood, if able to maintain a compliant partnership arrangement.

> The Common Brat must be carefully cultivated.

Communication

Welcome to the new aloofs!

Plugged in, ear-phoned, with eyes fixated on their phone screen, they move among us and between us and hear barely a word we say. Today's teens are the new aloofs. They control their boredom and their level of social involvement through technology. As a result they can be incredibly difficult to have a prolonged conversation with. For many parents the experience of raising hyper-connected teens is one of silence and disregard. Teens live in a world of conversational impoverishment. When a rare opportunity for a chat arises, most parents ruin it through overeagerness and an attempt to pack too much in to too little time. Let's try to provide you with a few pointers when those scarce occasions occur.

As if! Whatever! You are so random! That is so bizarre! OMG!

Communicating clearly with teens is a perilous undertaking. One moment they are monosyllabic and barely grunting at you, the next they have circumlocutory verbosity and are gushing a million words a minute. Whether chatty or barely verbal, there are a few things worth knowing about the importance of conversation.

The art of conversation

There is a Zulu saying that people are people because of other people. What connects us to others is love and conversation. A single conversation can change a life. Perhaps you can think of time when a comment so touched you, it echoed in your mind until it found a place in your heart. Perhaps there were words of comfort, of support or of understanding that you heard as a child that serve as a cloak against the chill winds of hurt that face us all from time to time.

> People are people because of other people.

Great conversations are like enchanting songs sung between people. Conversations harmonise and resonate and deepen our relationships. It is through conversation that we consolidate our identity and learn about who we are. Given the central space that conversations have in creating a meaningful and happy life, it seems that all of us should set ourselves the goal of becoming better conversationalists.

If you can think of some of the wonderful conversations you have had, it is probable that they had some of these features:

- People stopped what they were doing and really listened.

- Curiosity was piqued.

- Jealousy and competition were absent.

- Differences were seen as interesting rather than threatening.

- People felt able to be authentic and to show their vulnerabilities.

- Hurts might have been talked about, but faults were not.

> Conversations create a meaningful and happy life.

- Ideas and humour were in play.

The fine art of conveying a message, having it understood and then acted upon by another human being is an amazingly tricky business. When you are trying to influence a teenager, the mission becomes even more challenging.

We all have ongoing conversations with ourselves as well as with others. We can get into all sorts of trouble when we assume that what we say is the same as what people hear. It is important to know that:

- What is received is not necessarily what is sent.

- What is sent is not always what is meant.

What makes conversations even murkier is that it seems that men and women speak entirely different languages. The brains of teenage boys and girls are reasonably similar, but the way they use language is astoundingly different.

What conversations don't work with tricky teens?

Before we talk about the differences between the conversational styles of boys and girls, let's run through a few things parents regularly use that don't work.

The uninvited or unsolicited lecture This is a compelling habit. You can feel like you are imparting wisdom – the hard-earned lessons from the university of life. Ha! Perhaps you've noticed if you provide the same lecture in the same way again and again, you see their eyes roll. They go deaf on you. If you are absolutely determined to provide uninvited lectures, save yourself time by taping or podcasting your best lectures. Then you'll be able to say, 'Have a listen to this.' I can guarantee your lectures will be no less effective.

> It seems that men and women speak entirely different languages.

Appeals for loyalty or common sense 'After all we've done! Look how desperately worried we are! Anyone with any sense … If they told you to jump off a cliff would you do it?' Wringing your hands and looking concerned is not going to carry the day.

Self-sacrifice or self-denial This is the idea that parents should be stress martyrs who sacrifice their own lives to raise their kids. This takes many forms.

There might have been a pair of 'good' scissors in the home you grew up in. The idea of keeping the best things for special occasions often meant they were never used. Another example is the burnt chop syndrome, usually involving mothers who say things like, 'Don't worry dear, I'll have the burnt chop.'

Some parents stumble in from the outside world, lurch across the room, slump on the couch, look bleary-eyed at their teenager and ask, 'Have you done your homework, so you can grow up and be a success like me?' Then they wonder why their teens are unmotivated.

One of the most powerful things parents can do to promote wellbeing in their children is to live well. Make sure your teens see you enjoying yourself, catching up with friends and taking time to have great conversations. Show teens that life is worth living and success is worth attaining.

> Make sure your teens see you enjoying yourself.

Answering your own questions At times teens can be so sullen and uncommunicative that you can have a one-sided conversation in which you ask the questions and then fill in the answers. Be warned: this can sneak up on you. One day you walk away from a conversation with your teen and realise that only one person said anything at all.

Asking questions that don't work 'How was your day at school?' 'Who did you have lunch with?' They may not seem like it but these are incredibly complex questions for teens to answer. Let's peek behind the scenes and show you what happens for a boy when he's asked, 'How was your day at school?'

Q: 'How was your day at school?'	
Honest answer	**Simple answer**
Well, some of the learning wasn't bad but mostly it was pretty boring. At the moment, there is so much testosterone floating in my body I could strike up a romantic interest with a lamppost. Some of the girls in my class are pretty hot, even some of the teachers look good to me and given they are about my mother's age I'm worried that I'm weirdly perverted. I think I should go to the bathroom and put a 'Do Not disturb' sign on the door.	Not bad

Q: Who did you have lunch with at school today?'	
Honest answer	**Simple answer**
Well I was going to have lunch with Katrina but she thinks I've been talking to Susie too much so she's ignoring me as pay back. Susie and I talked. I'm kind of interested in someone at school but I think Susie is too. I'm not sure if I should stay interested or back off because Susie told me she was interested first. So now I'm not sure what I'm going to do. Maybe I'll ask Kylie what she thinks.	A few people

See, it's not easy being a teen. If parents want teens to talk to them, they need to ask questions that are easy to answer such as:

- 'What was the best thing that happened today?'

- 'Tell me something you learned today?'

Sometimes it is more productive to start with the negative and then move to the positive:

- 'What was the most boring class today?'
- 'What did you like least?'
- 'So what was the best part?'

Doing or saying the same thing over and over Some family interactions become so repetitive they lose any impact at all. Parents need to throw in comments out of left field to keep everyone on their toes.

Communication is a tricky business!

The difference between men and women in the way they communicate is often stark. For teens, it can be poles apart. These differences are illustrated by the contrasting interpretations of Bob Marley's song, 'No woman, no cry'. Many women interpret the song as about a tearful and upset woman being comforted by a loving and caring man in a time of need. Many men interpret the same song as No woman? No cry – that is, no problems.

While there are always exceptions to generalisations, it's useful to know how most men and most women use language. As we go through these differences, it will become clear that the fact that most relationships work at all is nothing short of miraculous.

Men are chasers and women are choosers and this is reflected in the way they talk to one another. Men use talk to gain attention and status, to be seen as the chosen one. Women use conversation to connect and maintain relationships. They are vigilant to shifts in nuances and tones. Females are well adapted to spotting men's evasions and exaggerations.

For men, language is about gaining respect and independence. Young men are especially vigilant for shifts in respect. The jostling and jockeying in male conversations is designed to answer the question, 'Do you respect me?' Jokes, stories and pranks are important to boys and men because they allow them to be centre stage and gain attention. It is extremely rare to see a woman at a barbecue call a few of the gals over and start sharing a joke.

For women, the art of conversation is about intimacy and connection. Behind much of their interactions are the questions 'Do you like me?' and 'Am I part of your group?' To build this connection through conversation, many women use discussions to emphasise similarity. For example, 'Oh yes, I've had that problem too!' Teen girls express this connection with, 'OMG that is so random, that is bizarre, we are so alike!'

Men and women talk about problems differently too. Women use problems to build similarity and closeness. If two women have a similar problem, they appear to be alike and will often link up as friends. Men look at problems as things to be minimised or solved. They might share problems and frustrations, but will often bond over minimising them.

Teen girl chat and teen boy chat

Girls speak two to three times more words than boys per day. By twenty months of age they have triple the vocabularies of boys. In schools, girls play games in which everyone gets a turn. Girls take turns twenty times more often than boys. Boys have games in which there are winners and losers.

Girls often form close-knit cliques with secret rules. They are on the phone with the door closed. Gossiping helps them cope with stresses and makes them feel they are not alone. Girls react to relationship distancing, boys to challenges to their authority.

> Boys need to be touched two to three times as much as girls.

Men mainly use vasopressin for bonding and relationships while women use oxytocin and estrogen. Vasopressin increases attention, protectiveness and tracking in men. Oxytocin is released in girls and even women with a twenty second hug – sealing the bond between huggers and trust. Boys need to be touched two to three times as much as girls to attain the same level of oxytocin. This is why raising a family of sons can feel like you are rearing a tribe of gorillas – they are all over one another, scuffling, pushing and shoving.

Advice for women speaking to men and boys

- Ask for advice and suggestions. Young men feel respected when their teachers ask them for help and their parents ask them for advice. However, women should, under no circumstance, feel obliged to implement anything they suggest!

- Try to see silence as contentment. Young men are often quietest when they are content and happy.

- Talk about activities rather than feelings.

- Use data (statistics, weird facts and numbers) rather than personal anecdotes.

- Don't ask for details. (They won't have them!) Mothers often make the following mistake with their sons.

  Mother: Is your friend having a birthday party?

  Son: Dunno

  Mother: What would he like as a present?

  Son: Dunno

  Mother: Would he like to come over for dinner one night?

  Son: Dunno.

- You will never truly understand the friendly world of rivalry and contest of boys and men. Women, you probably don't want to tune in to too much of all of this anyway!

- Conflict and difference do not always threaten intimacy. While women can interpret differences of opinion as threatening to the closeness of a relationship, this is not true for teen boys.

- Use short, sharp messages. Don't flood them with words or questions. Boys are fidgety and communicate in short bursts.

- Watching football is important and it is never an opportunity for a chat about feelings!

Young men will create challenge and rivalry out of almost anything. That is why they love lists. Whether it's the top ten songs featuring monsters or the top five supermodels or whether a team from an earlier era would beat a current team, competition and comparison is fun for them. Men can go and on about this kind of stuff while women sigh and reach for a good book.

Advice for parents speaking to daughters

- Drama, drama, drama! The female teen brain loves it. Expect it and don't think you can avoid some of it.

- Don't believe everything they say in arguments. As they are often more verbal than boys they can also say things to you that are more hurtful.

- Listening and reassurance can be enough. No parent has all the answers all the time. The good news is, you don't need to have all the answers. Fathers especially need to hear this: fathers do not need to solve all of their daughter's problems. Nor do mothers, for that matter.

- Let them know that you love them. Daughters will be reassured when supported emotionally and will often be willing to go to great lengths to please positive parents.

- In the first two weeks of their cycle, the high-octane hormone estrogen fuels sociability, outgoing interest, caring, looking at themselves in the mirror, chattiness as well as a few off-the-wall ideas.

- In the last two weeks of your daughter's cycle, progesterone dominates. Progesterone is the Greta Garbo of the hormone world and results in increased irritability and wanting to be alone. These hormones come in waves but in the progesterone phase, if some stress occurs, you often get meltdowns including yelling and slamming doors. Learn the patterns.

- Know her friends as well as you can. They will know her secrets and deals can always be struck if need be.

Advice for men speaking to women and girls

- Listen to understand before suggesting anything at all. When in doubt, *do not* suggest anything!

- Girls think if I just get 'it' right, I'll get the reaction I want. For example:

  - If I get 'it' right, he will love me.

  - If I do really well on this assignment my teacher will think I'm clever.

Fathers play a powerful role in shaping their daughter's life. Rather than aiming for compliance, teach her to be capable and clever. If you can gently show her what she can do, anxiety lessens and empowerment grows. Also help her learn that there is more than one way of getting things right.

- If a father stops responding to a daughter, she thinks he is distancing or she has done something wrong. She may panic. If you are feeling unresponsive or needing time alone, explain that you are feeling that way. If you have a headache and need some quiet time, let her know. Don't leave a daughter wondering and possibly blaming herself.

- Men don't read sadness in women well. Ask for details, who, what, where, when and how do you feel about that? Do not dismiss with a perfunctory, 'It will be all right' or 'Don't worry about it!'

- Don't try to joke them out of sadness. It doesn't work and it makes you look bad.

- Disclose. Use personal examples. If you don't have any, make them up.

- Notice details. They are important – earrings are not randomly chosen! Haircuts are for noticing. Shoes have symbolic meanings.

- Twenty seconds of hugging increases oxytocin in women.

- Learn that inter-dependence does not threaten freedom. You can rely on the women in your life. Confide in them and ask for their assistance – it won't compromise your masculinity.

- In arguments, don't defend yourself. Listen carefully for as long as it takes, then apologise sincerely if you're wrong.

Advice for parents speaking to sons

- Use unadulterated praise. Don't qualify (you did well but you could do better).

- Don't add ideas or suggestions, just praise. Don't say, 'Well you did really well and next time you could ...' Boys will only hear the second part of this statement and will go away feeling disrespected.

- Let him know that you love him and respect him. Tell him. Then tell him again. Keep telling him.

- Give options or choices wherever possible.

- Boys are more likely to have problems expressing feelings and be more liable to misinterpretations. Be direct. Be firm. Be fair and if you can, be funny.

- Always incorporate a wait time – so if you want something done by 5 pm, start suggesting it about two hours earlier and expect to have to remind him regularly over the intervening period.

- Boys are less resilient than girls and may be more romantic. Hurts run deep. Don't hover around them using a lot of words but stay nearby and be caring. The level of hurt that a teenage boy might feel after the break-up of a romantic relationship may surprise even him.

- Boys love the inside word, the cheat sheet. Boys like to score! Competition is fun for them.

- More acne is a clue that androgen levels are high. Increased androgen levels are associated with less empathy and more grumpiness. This may not be a good time for talking about feelings.

- Boys are often most communicative when horizontal – bedtime can be a good time for a chat.

Creating high impact conversations

Creating high impact conversations with teenagers is like fly-fishing in a stream of capricious fish. You may need to bait the hook with quite a few suggestions before you get a bite.

The number one most powerful tool to creating impactful conversations with teens is: *Drop everything to be available to talk*. When a teen wants to talk, be there. Don't allow phone calls, visitors, computers, television or anything else to interrupt you. Teens have the uncanny knack of wanting to talk at the least convenient times. This is not always coincidental. At times, it can be a test of how important you consider them to be. While we've all been guilty of saying to a child, 'Not now, later.' If we repeatedly do this, we telegraph to them that they are down our pecking order of priorities.

The second most powerful strategy is to be authentic and open your ears. If you sit with teenagers long enough, they will usually give you the answer. Don't rush in with solutions, just listen. In the age of interruption, true listening is a form of worship. We should all practise our listening skills. Try to listen in three ways:

- for what is being said

- for how it being said

- for what can be done about the issue.

> True listening is a form of worship.

The fine art of conversational fly-fishing

Skilled hypnotherapist Milton Erickson refined the use of language in wonderful ways. The parents of teenagers can also use these methods, as we will see.

Pacing involves tuning yourself to your teen's tempo. It can involve breathing at the same rate that they do. Matching them where they are now. Having matched their current behaviour, emotions and language for body signals, you are in a powerful position to understand the way they see the world. You are also in a position to take them where you want to go, or to lead.

Leading At the heart of influential language is presupposition. Presuppositions are the unsaid meanings and information in a sentence or phrases. For example, if someone were to say:

'Either now or in a moment, you will be able think of a time when a conversation has been important to you,' you are very likely to follow this instruction. This is because the first part of the sentence presupposes that you are going to do what has been suggested.

Along with presupposition is the idea of linking unrelated events. For example, you might say, 'As you go to the bathroom, I wonder if you could think creatively about this,' or, 'As you spread butter on your toast tomorrow morning, I wonder if you will think about what we've said.'

Here's another example of presupposition: 'You're a genius even though you've forgotten it, just like you've forgotten how you learned to walk.'

A further useful language technique is the 'yes set'. This method consists of making a series of statements that are undeniably true and then connecting them to a suggestion. For example, 'It looks to me like you are feeling a bit worried. (Pause – true) I guess there are other times you've felt worried too. (Pause – true.) When we get worried we all get tempted to give up on things. (Pause – true.) Then we learned that our worries eventually pass. (Suggestion – yes.) This method may feel artificial at first, but it is surprisingly effective.

> Seeding is knowing which bait to select.

Seeding   To revisit our fly-fishing analogy, pacing is knowing where the fish are. Leading them is enticing them with the possibility of bait. Seeding is knowing which bait to select. Seeding ideas often takes the form of embedded suggestions that can be used conversationally.

Remember that teens are tuned into emotions but are not especially aware of their thoughts. When a parent notices something about them, they have to reflect on whether to accept or reject the observation. To build this more powerfully, it is best to begin with giving positive feedback to your teen in the form of 'I noticed' comments. For example:

- I noticed you were really enjoying that show.
- I noticed you really worked hard at that.
- I noticed you felt energised when that happened.

Many teens don't get a great deal of positive feedback, so just providing several positive 'I noticed' comments a day can make a big difference.

'I notice' to 'You seem' to 'I wonder'

This will feel a bit odd at the beginning, so take it slowly and build up gradually. After you've started to use 'I noticed' comments, you can then add an 'and you seem' observation. For example:

- I noticed you worked really hard on that and you seem pleased with the result.
- I noticed you were a good friend to Sam and you seemed worried about her.
- I noticed you saying hello to that student and you seem more confident meeting people you don't really know.

Once this stops feeling totally weird and your teen has stopped looking at you as if your marbles are rattling around in your head, it's time to add the 'I wonder' portion. For example:

- I noticed you worked really hard at that drawing and you seemed so involved in it. I wonder if you are aware of how creative you are?

- I noticed you talking the problem through with your friend and you seemed to really care how they felt. I wonder if you've realised what a great friend you are?

Now you probably won't throw these comments casually into everyday conversation, but when you really want to amplify something that your teen has done and you want them to notice it too, this method works.

Computer addiction

The computer represents the edge of parental power. You no longer know many of your teen's friends because they don't physically enter your house. You no longer know all of your teen's interests because they are hidden. You don't know what photos, personal information, invitations to parties or details about your family have been posted online.

The cyber world offers even young teens a form of independence that even the most open-minded family a generation ago could have only dreamt of. Some parents feel so powerless in the face of computers that they have given up having any control while others flare into a rage at the sight of their teen at a computer and take it as a sign they are failing as a parent.

Neither position is helpful.

Most parents hold a view that there are two worlds: the 'real' world and the 'virtual' computer world. Some parents view the computer world as a frivolous waste of time. For most teens, however, there is no distinction between the virtual and the real world – both are indispensable. An online friend who has never been met physically can be just as influential as a neighbourhood friend. I once asked a teen what sport he played. He quite cheerily told me, 'Quidditch!

By the age of 21, teens will have spent 10 000 hours playing computer games.

The differences between teens and their parents in the ways they generally like to access and use information can be summarised as:

Many teens prefer	Many adults prefer
Rapid information	Slow intake of information
Staying connected	Having times of connection
24/7 availability	Times of unavailability
Pictures before text	Text before pictures
Hyperlinked multimedia information	Linear, sequenced information
Network with others first	Network with others after independent thought
Group think	Independent thinking
Learning just in time	Learning just in case
Instant gratification	Delayed gratification

Social media

Kids are as addicted to social media as humans are to oxygen.

When we ask students in schools what they consider to be the most important invention in all of history they often answer, the internet. One boy said, 'The wheel just goes round and round but the internet does everything!'

A lot of the so-called research in this area is a collection of biases, opinions and impressions, so we have to carefully sift out the sometimes over-hyped reporting about the cyber world to think clearly about this issue.

Social media explained

Twitter	I'm eating some cake
Facebook	I like cake
Foursquare/Urban Spoon	This is where I like eating cake
Instagram	This is a photo of my cake
Tumblr	Yum – a cake!
YouTube	Here is a video of me eating a cake
LinkedIn	My skills include cake eating
Pinterest	Here is a cake recipe
FM Last	I'm listening to 'Cake'
Google+	I'm a Google employee who eats cake

Celebrity culture The effect of using social media a lot is that teens become more self-centred and narcissistic. They are at the centre of every photo shoot. They are the celebrity at every event they attend. They are central to every discussion. For a generation raised to demand immediate gratification, social media is an invention made in heaven.

Top that! In the social media world, information grows old very, very quickly. This means that you need to update regularly or at least comment on others' updates. The pressure is high to make the funniest comment, post the wildest picture or make the most outrageous comment. Good news travels fast, but bad news spreads like wildfire. Rather like graffiti artists taking pride in their tags remaining intact or being copied, social media aficionados take pride in having their contributions shared by others. This adds to the urge to check in and see who is doing what with your latest addition to social media sites.

> For a teen ... social media is an invention made in heaven.

Signs there might be something to worry about

Here are a few pointers that could indicate your teen has a problem balancing their online life with their face-to-face life.

- They often stay online longer than intended/permitted.

- Family disputes about time spent online are becoming more common.

- They seem to prefer the excitement of the internet to time with friends or family.

- Their schoolwork suffers because of the amount of time they spend online.
- They become defensive or secretive when anyone asks them what they do online.
- They think that life without the internet would be boring, empty, and joyless.
- They often snap, yell or act annoyed if someone bothers them while they are online.
- They often choose to spend more time online over going out with others.
- They often seem depressed, moody, or nervous when offline, which goes away once they are back online.
- They deprive themselves of sleep in order to be online.

The world of instant comparisons

Want to feel like a loser? Hop on to Facebook on a dull day when no-one has really paid you much attention and you may be overwhelmed by envy and a sense that everyone is having a better time than you are. Add to that the social anxieties and gloominess that can afflict teenagers and you have a powerful mix for sadness and depression. Add a few negative comments from people about body shape, dating behaviour and general appearance and you have a potentially nasty situation. Place that same teen in the middle of the night, in a home where parents are asleep and there is no support. You have a tinderbox situation.

You mean this thing has an off button?

The idea of turning a computer off and doing something else is a foreign concept to many teens. The idea that the computer is an aspect of life parents should have some control over is very common among parents. It's a bit less popular among teens.

From teenager to screenager

Whether online activities will reshape the brains of people remains to be seen. Nevertheless, we can make a strong case that it is likely. Adolescence is a time when new pathways in the brain are being laid down. These pathways are built by repeatedly doing something. That is why we become more expert at something the more we practise it – and teens are certainly spending a lot of time practising being online. Some studies have indicated that teens spend eight and a half hours a day in front of some form of screen.

Most computer games give players a barrage of images and situations and call for lightning-fast decision-making. Most games reward fast, decisive action rather than thoughtful, considered strategy. The author

> Adolescence is a time when new pathways in the brain are being laid down.

Nicholas Carr calls this shift 'mind flit'. There is some research that computer usage changes brain activation patterns. One example of this is the way computers are changing the way young people read. Adults generally read from one third down and about one third of the way in and then scan in a Z pattern. Today's teens read in an F-shaped pattern.

Screens increase distractibility, skimming and scanning. Fast shifts in thinking online are mirrored in superficial thinking that leads teens to seek out the fastest, rather than the best or most creative, answer. Search engines, hyper-texts and links also encourage people to go on an endless hunt for new information. There is a dopamine surge when a new bit of information is found. Mind flit leads to idea juggling and multi-tasking. Stillness of mind is more evasive than ever.

Positive effects of social media and computer games

Teens are more intelligent than ever before. In fact they are considerably brighter than the average young person in 1950. Part of that amazing growth in intelligence can be attributed to playing computer games. Teens have developed hyperlinked minds. They know more about a whole lot of things. Computer games sharpen problem solving, hone social skills and fine-tune perception and response or reaction time. Social media can increase a sense of belonging, reduce racial differences by being connected with other teens across the world, and increase online empathy and helpfulness.

> Teens are more intelligent than ever before.

Can you overdose on technology?

Some teens become so fixated on social media that they have little time for anything else. School suffers. Physical health suffers.

They deprive themselves of sleep and social contact. Growing levels of obesity are another outcome, as are growing levels of shyness and social awkwardness, especially among young men. It is easier for some teens to be in the semi-controllable world of online interactions than to deal with the uncertainties and possible embarrassments of relationships.

Retreating into your bedroom and the excitement of online pornography may feel like a much safer bet than risking chatting someone up in the hope that you may get a romantic or sexual experience as a result. Porn addiction is an area we need to consider carefully without falling into moral outrage. The array, availability and intensity of online porn available may not seem all that different for the majority of teen young men than a stack of magazines under the bed. However, there is evidence to the contrary. There are quite of lot of reports of changes in teen sexual behaviour with reports of more boys wanting to imitate porn moves in their personal relationships. Also, the increase in awkwardness and shyness may be creating a shift away from seeking out relationships.

What parents can do

Computer addiction is like other addictions such as gambling, alcohol, drugs, eating, exercise or sex addiction. An addiction is a habit that reduces anxiety. Habits have set stages:

Cue → leads to change in neurochemical balance → triggers a routine or series of steps which → results in a reward

Let's go through an example. Lisa, 12 years of age, is having a tough time at school. Her best friend has recently left the school to move to another area and she is feeling lonely. Lisa tries to compensate by working harder to please her teacher. Last week she got a mark on a project that was much lower than she had hoped for. The same day she felt friendless at lunchtime. It seemed no one was available to chat to. Being on her best behaviour was hard, so by the time Lisa came home she was hungry and stressed. She had high levels of cortisol and adrenaline circulating in her body. After an argument at home, she retreated to her room and started playing computer games.

Computer game designers know how to engage players like Lisa. After an early experience of success in the computer game she was playing, Lisa was combating challenges that raised her levels of dopamine, she was gaining points and capabilities in the game. This form of positive feedback raises serotonin. By the time she reluctantly came down for dinner she was tired, but felt good. It is when things are challenging, scary or stressful for kids that computer games offer the most respite. A whiff of success on a tough day is an intoxicating experience.

Consequently, the addictiveness of computer games and social media are easy to understand.

1   They offer a break from reality.

2   It is an environment where young people can have success or acceptance.

3   Stressful, upset feelings can be replaced by feelings of competency, power and potency.

4   Dopamine and serotonin are feel-good chemicals.

Changing computer addiction

Any parent who tries to treat their teen's computer addiction will have an unwilling patient. Expecting teens to control their computer usage is like asking the advertising industry to self-regulate. Parents have three ways of controlling their teen's use of the net:

- sit down with them as they use it

- restrict access to sites offering violence and sexual images

- restrict the amount of time young people can access the net each day.

Digital diet

Addicts crave things. A computer-addicted teen when denied total access will throw every trick in the book at you. It will take some hard-headed parenting for teens to turn off their digital identity and turn on themselves instead. Don't expect much change in a month and expect no gratitude. Weaning teens from too much computer time requires your presence and determination.

Start by helping the teen earn computer access by completing specific tasks – homework, sports and social activities. Realise that once they get on the computer, the likelihood of any of these tasks being completed is close to zilch. Gradually try to re-ignite non-computing challenges such as sport, art or music. Keep them as busy as you can. Socialise more and help them focus more directly on schoolwork. Older teens can also be encouraged to take up part-time work. You may also like to read the issue on reclusive teens to help your thinking on this topic.

While most behaviours are changeable by implementing a six-week process, computer addiction is an exception. The level of compulsion some teens have for the computer is such that weaning them off it doesn't work. Discussion doesn't work. Providing distractions doesn't work. Providing rewards and punishments doesn't work. What works is parents finding technological ways to block teens from accessing the internet between certain hours.

Use technology to control technology

The suggestion to keep technology under parental supervision by having computers in the main rooms of the house no longer works because the modern computer is the smart phone. Each computer, phone and tablet in your home has a unique number. The way it links to the internet is through an airport device or a router. Parents can enter their router and specify the hours that each device has access to the internet.

> Weaning a teen off a computer addiction doesn't work.

For example, if you want to block your teens' laptop and phone from having access to the internet between 10 pm and 7 am, you can do this. The process of doing this varies for different systems and no doubt will change over time, so the best way to find out more about this would be to search about how to restrict internet access on your specific device.

Confidence

It is not because things are difficult that we do not dare. It is because we do not dare that things are difficult.

Seneca

Confidence is one of the most powerful, and one of the most elusive, qualities that leads to success in life. If someone could work out a way to manufacture confidence and sell it, they would be rich overnight. But confidence does not come in a tablet or a supplement and it especially doesn't come in a bottle. Some teens find their confidence lowers as they progress through school. They give up believing they can do anything and become wary of trying new things. Building confidence means that we develop the courage to try out new things.

> Some teens find their confidence lowers as they progress through school.

Confidence is not talent

Sometimes we can be tricked into thinking that if only we were more skilled, talented, beautiful and generally fantastic and wonderful, we would feel more confident. Baloney! I have worked with many highly successful people who lack confidence – top models who believe they lack beauty, sports stars who have had a lapse of confidence. The same applies to those who experience intellectual success.

Almost all of us approach new activities with a slight apprehension, usually followed by bewilderment and confusion. Our first attempts may be feeble but if we persist, we often gain a sense of mastery. If someone rescues us when we are bewildered, we learn that someone else can do what we cannot. This is why parents rescuing teens when they are struggling with a new activity is toxic to confidence building.

Trust your teen

There are several steps to creating and building confidence. Firstly, trust builds confidence. One of the best ways of communicating your trust is to ask your teen for help. Requesting assistance communicates to them that you regard them as capable and competent. Asking your teenagers to cook with you can be a good place to start.

Live a bold and adventurous life

One of the best ways to help your teen develop confidence is to show them how to live an expansive life in which you do different things, try new food and attempt new things. Encourage adventure by planning family outings that take everyone out of their comfort areas. Whether it is orienteering, volunteering or staying in youth hostels, teens need to be shown that there is a bigger world out there. This is particularly important for teens who want to cling to the safety of a few close friends and become tentative about venturing far beyond that group.

Trust your intuition

The world often provides teens with conflicting messages. Helping teens to weigh information and to see that some of the information they receive may not be what it seems is a good start. Becoming a discerning consumer involves being able to analyse and decode thousands of messages directed at young people every day. Help them to learn that not everyone has their best interests at heart; some just want them to buy stuff.

> Get teens to practise trusting their intuition and hunches.

Talking about moral dilemmas often involves encouraging teens to think in different ways. Involve teens in conversations where they gather and analyse information from different perspectives before making a decision. Once they've considered the options, get them to practise trusting their intuition and hunches.

Turning molehills into monsters

When you avoid something you fear, your fear grows. What is avoided looms larger and appears more daunting, but what is attempted, lessens in size. While it might seem like a kindness to help teens opt out of things they are fearful of doing, mostly it just makes them more fearful.

Teens typically amplify the social consequences of failing at anything. They say things like:

- 'That is so lame.'

- 'That would be so embarrassing.'

This hides a fear of failure. What they are really expressing is fear. Some teens are so cautious and fearful that they act as if trying anything even slightly adventurous would be tantamount to social humiliation. We all need to learn at some stage in life to get over ourselves and have a go. Encourage your teen to embrace new opportunities and experiences. Some teens need parents who bossily say, 'For goodness sake. Just try it. If you don't have a go, you never know whether you'll like it.' Others may be more responsive to gently pointing out that they may miss an important opportunity if they don't try something.

> Avoidance is really a fear of failure.

Don't wait to feel confident

Remind teens that no one is confident at everything all the time. We all experience hesitations and setbacks. Encourage your teen to be bold and confident about 80 per cent of the time. In many areas of life, it is the predominant pattern that counts in the long term.

First past the post isn't always the best

There is a myth that has been circulating for years now that the child or teenager who can do something at the youngest age will be the best at it in the long term. It isn't true. There are considerable advantages in being a little bit older when you start new activities.

Set probability goals

Some teens think if they can't get something right 100 per cent of the time the first time they try it, there is no point doing it. It doesn't matter how many times you point to accomplished people and mention the numbers of hours it has taken for them become successful. It doesn't matter how clearly you tell them that no one starts off as an expert. These tricky teens believe that they should be the exception. For these all-or-nothing teens, we set probability goals.

A probability goal is a challenge that includes an error margin. For example, a parent might say to a teen, 'Let's see if you can throw a ball into a hoop on the ground 7 times out of 15 throws.' As the teen becomes more skillful, we might then increase the challenge of the task by moving the hoop further away and say, 'OK, it's harder now. Let's see if you can throw the ball into the hoop 9 times out of 20.' Probability goals are less threatening than a goal of getting it right first time. Probability goals help us learn how to challenge ourselves and also make it less likely that we will give up if we don't get 100 per cent first time.

> Focus on your teen's strengths.

Little steps to giant leaps

When we focus on our strengths, we build the confidence to tackle areas where we are not so capable. It's easy and tempting to focus on practising things we already do well. It's fun and the pay-off is immediate. The problem is that confidence is built when we stretch ourselves and practise skills that we are not so competent in.

This is known as 'deliberate practice' and involves setting aside time to practise skills we are not proficient in.

Most highly skilled and confident people deliberately practise skills. They put themselves into challenging situations so they can become more skilled. Top golfers often put golf balls into the trickiest part of a bunker so they have to develop the skills to make those shots. People only learn to deliberately practise skills that they are not so good at when someone has clearly told them that they believe in them and that mistakes are the only way to get better at something. If we can't learn to make mistakes, we can't learn to improve. People who don't make mistakes don't usually make anything.

Build a have-a-go culture

Teens often express their insecurities by claiming that they can't do something or by comparing themselves negatively with others – 'I am the world's worst dancer' or 'I'm no good at maths.' When teens makes comments like these, acknowledge their feelings and help them to express them verbally. Ask what makes them feel that way. Accept their fears or insecurities as genuine, but don't agree with their self-assessment. For example, you might say, 'I get it that you're struggling at maths. How can we work on that?'

Encourage your teen to devote their life towards looking for the best in themselves and in others. Focus on successes, skills and abilities. Be resolutely positive and follow the role model of Thomas Edison who, after trying 10 000 times to develop an electric light bulb said, 'I have not failed. I've just found 10 000 ways that don't work.'

Depression

About 20 per cent of people experience depression at some time in their lives. That means that almost every family has someone with depression at times. Unfortunately, once someone has experienced depression, they are at a far greater risk of feeling that way again. The earlier you experience depression the greater the risk, usually. This is why preventing depression in children and teens is so important. While we can't protect everyone from depression, there are things that we can do to make it less likely.

> Almost every family has someone with depression at times.

Sadness is not always bad

Everyone loves being happy but being sad at times is not such a bad thing. Sadness gives us time for thinking things over, sometimes regretting things we have done. It can help us to resolve to be better people. Feelings of sadness, loss, disappointment and setbacks are just part of life. Without them, we don't live whole lives. Remorse and regret often kick-start reflection that helps us learn some of life's most important lessons. If we treat times of sadness as a catastrophe to be fixed as quickly as possible, we risk missing some of the lessons it has to teach us and do not grow into fully-fledged adults.

We all want our kids to be happy but know that there will be times they will be sad. It's important that teens know having emotional ups and downs is normal and they won't be happy all the time. All feelings pass and realising we can learn from the whole range of feelings, sadness included, is part of being human.

Depression is more than just sadness, however. It is ingrained, entrenched and bleak. Sadness is generally short-term and shifts as circumstances change. Depression is longer-lasting and it is more like a pit the teen can't seem to get out of no matter how hard they try. Depression affects mood, energy, sleep, appetite and libido.

What we deny or try to suppress in ourselves seeks expression. Help your teen accept that there will be times in their lives when they feel sad. These times are opportunities to reflect and consider whether we should be doing things differently. While painful, they don't last forever. If we don't accept sadness, we don't deal with some of our issues and that puts us at a higher risk of depression.

Optimal growing conditions

Try to identify some of the major sources of stress in your teen's life and develop systems to deal with them. If you can't avoid stressful situations, at least develop a de-compression strategy. This is a way of winding down after being revved up. Going for a walk, doing some exercise and being active are some of the best ways.

If you've ever bought a plant from a garden nursery, you might have noticed it comes with a plastic sleeve that gives instructions. It might say, 'Plant in rich soil in partial shade and provide lots of water.' It specifies the optimal growing conditions for that plant. We all have our own optimal growing conditions. Some people love to be in a swirl of activity all of the time.

Others love physical challenges. Still others like a more peaceful lifestyle. Whatever works for you, works for you. Most teens are yet to find their optimal growing conditions. Most are so busy reacting to the world around them that they haven't learned how to create the conditions that bring out the best in themselves.

Parents can do two really useful things for teens in relation to optimal growing conditions. The first is to consider what your own personal growing conditions are and surround yourself with them. Discuss what you are doing with your teen. They might look at you disparagingly as you sprawl on the couch surrounded by chocolates and listen to that favourite song, but it's important that they understand what you are doing.

> Teens do what they see other people do.

Secondly, when you think you have identified one of your teen's optimal growing conditions, remark on it: 'I notice you get really fired up and happy after you've played badminton.' Identifying and highlighting this observation about their optimal growing conditions to your teen makes it more likely that they will replicate them when they encounter stressful times.

Take your headphones off and talk to someone Find some good friends. Friends are true treasure. Along with family, having a few good friends who we can talk things over with enriches our lives and protects us in difficult times. Encourage teens to broaden their social networks by talking to people. It takes courage to say hello to people you don't know.

Teens do what they see other people do. It's important for your teen to see you chatting to people you know, saying hello to some people you don't know, greeting people and being outgoing. Don't be discouraged when your teens roll their eyes and describe you as a social try-hard. You're doing it for both of you.

Read books   At the risk of sounding curmudgeonly, if you don't create a bigger world for yourself, all you've got is what's happening today. People who don't read books have only one life. Readers can access thousands of lives. Books fire up the imagination, they immerse people in alternative ways of living life and ignite dreams. If you can't dream it, you can't be it. If you can't inspire your teen to read books, help them create a bigger world by seeing movies, travelling, mixing with different types of people and going on adventures.

Eat healthily   What we eat changes our moods. In countries where people eat low levels of fish, depression levels are higher. Fish contains a fatty acid known as EPA, which is lacking in people with depression. Fatty acids are also found in flaxseed, walnuts and chia seeds. These are good fats and they can guard against depression. Whole grain oats have been shown to help with depression as they contain folic acid and B vitamins. This helps with a slow release of energy versus the crash and burn of blood sugar levels. Food high in selenium which is found in meat, fish and cereal grains decreases symptoms of depression. Leafy greens have magnesium, which helps with depression and also helps you sleep better.

> We experience 'flow' when we get involved in an activity that captivates us.

Sources of 'flow'   We experience 'flow' when we get involved in an activity that captivates us. At the end of these types of activities people often think, 'Where did the time go?' There are many sources of flow – computer games, sports, drawing, dancing, reading, swimming and surfing are some. These are the things that you do that absorb you and take you away from your day-to-day cares and worries.

Losing yourself in a few pleasurable activities that challenge you is highly protective against depression. Children are often wonderful creators of flow. They play, pretend and immerse themselves in activities for hours on end. However, many teens and adults feel that they are too grown up to play. Encourage your teen to be playful, jokey and to see quirky aspects of life. If you need an excuse to play, remember that play promotes mindfulness, awareness, creativity and imagination.

Belong to the karma club For one week, decide to increase good-will in the world by doing something positive for someone else. Pick someone you know and 'knock their socks off'. Give them compliments, greet them exuberantly and take time to be with them. You'll be amazed at how much benefit you get from increasing someone else's happiness.

> Pick someone you know and 'knock their socks off'.

I love watching teens when they do this. Sometimes we call it 'positive shock therapy'. They are interested in the reactions they receive. What they also get is a sense of their power to change the world. Most of us don't change the world by curing the common cold; most of us do it incrementally. We influence one person, who influences another and so on. Goodwill, compliments and kind gestures are contagious.

Be grateful and lucky Being grateful and appreciative protects teens against depression. Even people who have had rotten things happen to them can rise above them. They usually do this by deciding to be lucky. While we can focus on the things that have upset us, most of us have many things and people to be grateful for. Focusing on that part of your life and deciding that you are lucky makes an enormous difference to your life.

Get enough sleep and rest   Getting enough sleep is one of the most powerful ways we can protect our teens against depression. The structures in the brain that support the most powerful antidepressant, serotonin, are built and rebuilt between the sixth and the eighth hour of sleep. About a third of teenagers are chronically sleep deprived. Over 60 per cent of people who sleep five or less hours a night end up obese and depressed. If your teen is having difficulty sleeping, get them to:

- decrease caffeine consumption late in the day
- decrease sugar in their diet
- go to bed at the same time every night and wake up at the same time every morning
- avoid late nights
- avoid naps, especially after 4 pm
- avoid spicy, sugary or heavy foods before bedtime
- have the room at a comfortable temperature (some teens want to heat up the room and sweat the night away)
- block out distracting noise
- don't sit in bed while studying – get in the habit of reserving it for sleep
- drink warm milk before bed as it's high in tryptophan, which aids sleep
- try relaxation methods before sleeping
- write out a to-do list for the next day before getting into bed
- have a pre-sleep ritual like reading or a warm bath

- switch off the electronics, especially phones and backlit tablets

- don't use energy drinks to give you a boost.

Allow them to have a few days of feeling tired. Help them to wake up early and go out into the morning sunlight. Gradually, normal sleep patterns will resume.

Get some exercise   Exercise decreases stress hormones such as cortisol and increases endorphins (the happy chemicals). It also helps release dopamine, adrenaline and serotonin, which work together to make you feel good. Endorphins are a hormone-like substance produced in the brain. They function as the body's natural painkillers. During exercise, endorphins can leave you in a state of euphoria with a sense of wellbeing. The most effective type of exercise for the release of endorphins is cardiovascular exercise and aerobics. Moderate exercise for ten minutes a day is enough to improve your mood and increase energy but it is suggested that you do thirty minutes per day.

Laugh more   Laughter raises our levels of serotonin and dopamine. Make a point of watching TV shows or movies that make you laugh. Share funny stories and jokes with friends. People report that laughing even when they don't feel happy improves their mood and sense of wellbeing.

When should I worry about my teen?

In the childhood and teenage years, depression can be harder to pick because it is obscured by heightened emotions and times of grumpiness. Some signs of depression are:

- loss of interest in usual activities
- low motivation – their get up and go has got up and gone
- increased use of drugs and alcohol
- sleep problems
- changes in energy levels – sluggish or agitated and restless
- changes in eating patterns – uninterested in food or over-eating
- speaking about death and hopelessness
- increased and inexplicable irritability
- your own feelings of anxiety about your child.

It's worth getting help if your teen appears depressed. Your own life is too precious to waste worrying. However, getting your teen to see someone or get help can be tricky. A possible way to make this happen is to say, 'I'm worried about you and I want you to come with me to see someone so that I can work out whether I should be worried or not.' Try to find a good local psychologist, psychiatrist or doctor who can relate to young people. Persist in finding someone your teen likes and can relate to.

Know how to make yourself happy and miserable

As a parent of a tricky teen you need to be a moodologist. You need to know that the majority of happiness and misery in people's lives is created by themselves. On the next few pages are some pointers to making yourself either happy or miserable. Learn these and teach them to your teen. One mother placed

'How to be happy' on one wall in her toilet and 'How to be miserable' on the opposite wall to remind herself and her teens that they had a choice every day.

How to be happy

The art of making yourself happy is something we can all learn and practise. No one is happy 100 per cent of the time. Life has its ups and downs. Even so, there are some sure-fire ways to increase your happiness.

1   Don't wait to see if you are having a good time

Instead of going places and waiting to see if it is fun, decide in advance to have fun regardless of the circumstances. Enjoy the day regardless of the weather. Make the most of the occasion regardless of the company.

2   Go outside and play

You were told to do this as a kid and I'm telling you to do it again – play more. Go for walks, throw a dog a stick, skip, sing loudly or imagine yourself to be a spy passing through enemy territory. Whatever does it for you. Make a promise to play more.

3   Develop deep friendships

Friends are your true wealth. Value them and see them regularly. Let them know how important they are to you. Most people only have two close friends so don't fool yourself into believing you are less popular than most people.

4   Increase the closeness of extended family

Keeping in close contact with your family gives you a support base in difficult times and strengthens your sense of where you come from. Feeling you belong in a family is a powerful way of being happy.

5   Play to your strengths

Have a long, hard look at yourself. What are you good at? Make a commitment to develop your skills, talents and abilities as much as you can. If you don't develop your own unique talents, the world misses out.

6   Seek out groups that value what you have to offer

Finding the niche where your abilities are valued is the basis of success.

7   Avoid social groups where your unique attributes are not valued

Not everyone is going to like you or think you could amount to much. Get used to it. Accept that it is so, and then get out of their way.

8   Live in the dreamtime

Find and follow your passions. Dream big dreams and make a promise to yourself to live a wonderful life.

9   Laugh a lot more

Find people, shows, books, films and situations that make you laugh and surround yourself with them.

10   Have something bigger than yourself to believe in

Think about the contribution you can make while you are on this planet – and do it.

11   Love as much as you can – and then love some more

How to make yourself miserable

Being miserable is an art form. There are many ways of achieving it. A few sure-fire ways are below.

1   Wait for the situation to be right before having a good time

One of my favourite Chinese proverbs is 'People who wait for roast duck to fly into mouth, will wait long time.' Put off having a great life until you have the right job/house/partner/friend is a great way of putting off life all together.

2   Compare yourself to others

Spend hours thinking about how much more beautiful, happy, intelligent, creative, insightful and wonderful everybody else is compared to you. Think that glossy people who are featured in glossy magazines have glossy lives despite lots of evidence to the contrary.

3   Give others the power to control your life

Don't do the things you want to do. Let other people choose your life directions and priorities. This allows you to avoid responsibility. When you end up miserable (and believe me you will!) blame the people you let make the decisions.

4   Try to make other people happy

Try to fix other people or spend your life trying to please them. Base your life decisions on what other people will think of you rather than what you want to do.

5   Feel it is better to avoid rejection than to love

Play safe. If you don't try to love people you can't be let down or hurt. Resign yourself to a life of perpetual disappointment.

6   Talk yourself out of stuff you really would like to do
Spend time telling yourself you can't do things because you are
not smart enough or talented enough and you really can begin to
believe that if you don't try, you can't fail.

7   Believe you don't deserve to be happy

8   Say yes when you mean no
It's nice to be helpful and agreeable but if you say yes to things
you don't want to do, you can end up feeling really bad about
yourself or resentful of people. Long-term resentment turns into
bitterness.

Drugs and alcohol

Tune in, turn off and drop in! There are three types of young
people who use drugs – experimenters, the socially disconnected
and self-medicators.

Experimenters   Most teens try alcohol or drugs but don't have
major problems with them. Most teenagers experiment at some
point with some form of drug. Alcohol use is more the norm than
the exception. Figures vary from country to country and area
to area, but about 28 per cent of Year 12 students drink alcohol
regularly, many binge drinking when they do so. More girls than
boys smoke tobacco. At least 25 per cent (and probably many
more) young people experiment with marijuana.

Socially disconnected These teens use alcohol and drugs to gain social acceptance. They find that having an intoxicant relieves them of the social anxiety associated with mixing and talking to other teens. These teens are more in need of social strategies and skills in chatting up the teens they are interested in, than in drug or alcohol education. Try to help them to understand that being fairly sober or mentally with-it will increase their chances in the romantic/sexual stakes. This helps curb their usage. The sexiest teen at the party is not the one who is vomiting. They need parents or other adults to talk to them about picking up and interacting with other teens successfully.

> Be firm and know when to get help.

Self-medicators Self-medicating teens use alcohol and drugs to escape emotional pain and don't believe they can lead happy or successful lives without them. If you feel your teen falls into this category, seek professional assistance or advice.

Be firm. It is OK to set rules about drug and alcohol use in your home. It's also OK to be forceful about directing young people towards help if they need it. Drug users rarely see that they have a problem.

Should parents feel it is their fault?

There are many factors that lead to young people using drugs. Parents shouldn't feel directly to blame, but should take on the job of helping their child to avoid developing a drug problem. At the same time, parents should always think about the messages their own behaviour sends about drug and alcohol use (including alcohol and cigarettes). Try to keep discussions about drugs and alcohol free from conflict. If a young person is using drugs you can be stern or even disapproving, but it is too late for anger and dramatics.

Parents shouldn't feel that they need to accept young people's drug use. In fact, too accepting an attitude may give the false impression that you don't care. Ask your teen how they think using drugs helps them. Then, ask yourself how you are showing your teen ways of leading a happy and fulfilling life without drugs. Show them that we can have celebration without intoxication. There's little point telling teenagers horror stories about drugs. Horror stories sometimes backfire and parents become dismissed as out of touch and falsely concerned.

Horror message about drugs and alcohol	Common teen interpretation
If you drink and drive, you're an idiot.	If you drink and drive, you're a legend.
Alcohol is a depressant.	Not in my experience!
Ecstasy is mixed with crushed glass/rat poison/evil things that make you drop dead.	All those people dancing at festivals are not dropping dead.
Smoking gives you lung cancer.	I'm a teenager. I'll worry about that when I'm old.
LSD will make you think you can fly and you may jump off a building and die.	A cool way to go!

Alcohol

The drug to worry about the most is alcohol. Alcohol usage increases the probability of violence, accidents and life-threatening risk-taking. It's the most immediately dangerous drug for young people. Teens process alcohol differently from adults. They can drink more and for longer periods than adults. When they drink, teens get as silly as adults but they don't get as sleepy. By the stage that most adults are ready for a good lie down and snooze after a few drinks, teens are up and ready to down even more drinks. Teenagers also seem to be more vulnerable than adults to memory blackouts as a result of drinking. As teens mainly drink at parties and sometimes with other teens secretly, the fact that they can't remember what they have done is concerning.

What protects young people against drug problems?

Making sure your teen has the possibility of a fulfilling life is the strongest antidote to problematic drug use. Feeling that your parents love and care for you, that you fit in at school and having a group of friends – not all of whom use drugs – are factors that protect young people.

When to get worried

Always try to educate young people about the dangers of alcohol and drug misuse and help them make educated choices about the substances they use.

Some indications that it is time to involve an outside professional are:

- when there is drug or alcohol use at school
- when there are ongoing school absences due to alcohol or drug usage
- when drug or alcohol use occurs when truanting from school
- when other family members express concern about the young person's drug use
- when there is evidence that the young person is mixing drugs to enhance their potency.

If any of these are occurring, seek professional assistance from a mental health or drug and alcohol specialist.

Talking to teens about alcohol

Our attitudes around drinking are seriously conflicted.

We deplore random violence in our streets	but	We don't address the alcohol consumption that causes it.
We want to preserve our children's childhood	but	If they pester us enough we will give them a few drinks to take to a party.
We fear the consequences of young people mixing drinking and driving	but	We don't ensure they stay sober enough to get home safely.

| We deplore sexual assault and date rape | **but** | We seem to forget this occurs in the context of alcohol and drugs at parties. |
| We want our kids to have a great life | **but** | We don't question it when they feel the only way they can do this is to have a few drinks first. |

We live in a society that has forgotten that you can have a celebration without intoxication. With this level of mixed messages floating around, teens are not going to be convinced not to drink alcohol unless parents take a clear, strong stand.

Ten quick reasons why teens should not use alcohol

1   The growing brain is more easily damaged by alcohol.

2   It is against the law.

3   It is against the law.(Yes, I know I just said that, but I wanted to repeat it so you don't glide over it.)

4   People who drink as teenagers are more likely to become problem drinkers when they become adults.

5   Teenagers process alcohol differently. Adults get sleepy after too many drinks. Teens are up and firing and ready to do all manner of risky things.

6   Teens don't know when to stop drinking. Most teens binge when they drink.

7 Alcohol-related traffic crashes are a major cause of death among young people. Alcohol use is also linked with teen deaths by drowning, suicide and homicide.

8 Teens who use alcohol are more likely to be sexually active at earlier ages, to have sexual intercourse more often, and to have unprotected sex than teens who don't drink. Teen parties can be dangerous places to be if you are intoxicated.

9 Young people who drink are more likely than others to be victims of violent crime, including rape, aggravated assault and robbery.

10 Teens who drink are more likely to have problems with schoolwork and school conduct.

What teens want from drinking alcohol

Some teens want to drink at parties to get smashed, off-their-face, rat-faced blotto. These are the people who are most likely to become problem drinkers as adults. Permissive parents who provide alcohol for them signal to them that getting blind drunk is acceptable. Other teens want to drink at parties because it will lessen their anxiety. Parties are filled with romantic possibilities and teens are mostly pretty anxious about picking up.

Tips for talking with your teen

Teens need to know where you stand on this issue. Be clear and unambiguous. Recognise that it is tough. It's much tougher in this country not to drink than to drink. Say, 'I'm going to ask you to do something tough. I know this is hard and I know you probably won't agree. I don't want you to drink alcohol until you are 18.' If it helps, use one of the ten reasons why alcohol should not be used by under 18-year-olds to justify your statement.

Expect disagreement. Expect to hear 'everyone else is', 'all the other parents let their kids drink,' 'you are so old fashioned,' 'you're the worst parent,' and 'you can't stop me' or 'you don't love me.' Don't expect your teen to be swayed by the strength of your argument the first time you raise this issue. There is no need for you to answer their claims in detail, so don't get drawn into a long-winded dispute. If it seems likely to become an argument say, 'You know my position. Let's discuss it again when you've had a chance to think it over.' Then move away. If the discussion is calmer, you might consider outlining the consequences if you find they've been drinking alcohol.

> Expect to hear 'all other parents let their kids drink' ...

Generally teens will go away sulking and scheming and then come back to make a further argument in favour of drinking alcohol. Usually their new argument is based on their fears of social rejection as a dry, unfashionable nerd. Ostracism and ridicule will be envisaged. Stick to your argument. Eventually, you will get to a point where you can plan strategies for handling the pressure to drink at parties. Remind your teen that it's possible to have fun without drinking.

Things teens can say to explain why they are not drinking at parties

1 My parents would kill me.

2 I have a rare medical condition.

3 I have a performance tomorrow.

4 I have an allergic reaction to alcohol that requires hospitalisation.

5 I have made a deal with my parents that if I don't drink until I'm 18 I get a lot of money.

6 I'm hung over from last night.

7 I'm on a diet.

8 I'm on medication that reacts really badly with alcohol.

9 I'm the designated driver (if older).

10 I'm in a training phase and we've agreed as a team not to drink until after the finals.

11 I've decided not to drink. (This is the hardest because some teens will want to question or influence your teen's decision.)

Girl smarts

Teenage girls can be trickier than teenage boys, especially for their mothers. This is partly because a girl has to work to differentiate herself from her mother while a boy is already different. There are a few strategies that help most teenage girls to thrive.

We're all in this together

Girls generally like people who like them. They want to fit in and be part of the group. They want to do well. Many girls like to be prepared. For this reason, parents should reveal plans in advance. Give directions the day before. Give them advance notice of forthcoming events. Some boys need this as well, though many boys are more likely to engage when you spring it on them.

Override the cliques

Some girls waste a lot of time worrying needlessly about relationship issues. Relationship divisions are toxic to girls. Encourage your daughter to have multiple groups of friends and to not allow other girls to be excluded. Override the cliques yourself. While your daughter may have one or two special friends, impress upon her the need to include other people and to treat all people well.

> Encourage your daughter to have multiple groups of friends.

Inclusive is better than exclusive

Select schools that don't allow girls to splinter into set groups. Good schools move girls about and get them interacting with a variety of other students, not just their special best friends. If allowed to control the social interaction, girls can be merciless and organise vendettas against other girls. If this occurs, you need to call out the behaviour and give clear consequences. Teenage daughters will respond when you are clear about your expectations of them socially. If your daughter is the target of a vendetta, let her school know and plan actions to overcome this together. Good schools take these matters seriously and act on them.

Praise more than you think you need to

Just as boys love it if you tell them are legends, geniuses and are brilliant, girls initially want to know that you like them. They are more responsive than boys to facial cues so make eye contact, smile and nod positively more when talking to girls. Girls who have a sense that you like them and are interested in them will want to collaborate with you.

Value them and they become heroines

Have a clear set of values. Live them and insist on your daughter living by them too. Talk about women who have had a powerful impact on the world and establish community projects (not just fund raisers) that show them they can make a difference. It's especially powerful when fathers do this with their daughters. Fathers can strongly promote their daughters' sense of competence. When a father asks his daughter for advice and suggestions it indicates that he respects her intellect and communicates to her that other boys and men should do the same.

Teach self-reliance

Once teen girls are secure in the knowledge that you like and love them, it's useful to move them from impressing you towards self-reliance. We want to help create empowered young women rather than compliant ones. To do this you need to create a non-judgemental environment in which they can take risks. The world sometimes communicates to teenage girls that their role is to wait: wait to be asked out, wait for the first kiss and wait to be chosen. Snow White, Cinderella and Sleeping Beauty weren't doing much until the Prince showed up. Parents should strongly convey the message that girls can instigate events and actions.

The desire that many girls have to 'get it right' can quickly topple into anxiety and perfectionism. Perfectionist girls may constantly seek reassurance that they are doing the right thing. Teach them to trust their instincts and do what they think is right. Most girls will do what is asked of them, but they may be less likely to realise that they have acquired a skill. They may be more likely to focus on pleasing a parent and attribute successes to having impressed you rather than improvements in their own skills and capabilities. Help them develop a resume of acquired skills. Teach girls that everyone can get smarter. Don't allow them to avoid trying things. Encourage them to have a go and live by their wits.

> Girls can instigate events and actions.

Girls need quiet time

Many girls are intensely social and they can over-identify with their friends. The world of social comparisons can be harsh for girls and they can discount their own abilities and creativity. Try to create times for your daughter to be alone, times when she can think, be quiet and creative.

The answer is the answer

Girls often think that if hard work pays off, working longer and harder will always result in more success. Teach them to work smarter.

They also need to know it makes no difference how much work you put into completing a project if the outcome is wrong. Glitter pens and beautiful covers are lovely but don't hide inadequate work. When girls have projects or homework to do but can't get going, give them a time trial: 'I want to see how much you can get done in twenty minutes.' This helps overcome procrastination.

Don't dampen high-energy girls

Some girls are naturally high-spirited with lots of energy. Make sure you don't subtly indicate that they should be quiet and more docile. Girls are often given implicit messages such as don't get too excited, don't run too fast, don't overdo it or get too tired. Don't be too you.

Girls often try to gain acceptance through being similar to others and that can squash the spirit of some girls and engender over-compliance. Talk about women who have been rebels. Even better, be a bit of a rebel yourself. Know that it is easy to disempower girls by showing them how to do things rather than getting them to solve issues. Don't be too helpful. As girls often want the 'right' answer, it is tempting for parents to try to alleviate their anxiety by helping them. It is far more empowering if you provide ideas and suggestions, but allow her to struggle though to find her own answers.

> Be a bit of a rebel yourself.

Don't be critical of their decision-making processes. Even helpfully suggesting, 'Have you thought about ...' can breed self-doubt. Keep in mind that daughters will need to make a few wrong decisions in order to learn the skill of self-reliant decision-making.

Give girls special access to technology

Encourage computer use. Boys often get plenty of screen time. Girls use computers for social networking, but may need to be encouraged to complete tasks, conduct research and seek data on computers.

> Illustrate the relevance of science in their world using real-life scenarios they can relate to.

Make mathematics hands on

Some girls become intimidated by mathematics and science subjects. Having female teachers in these areas helps. Making mathematics and sciences hands on and people-oriented will keep girls engaged. Use models, manipulatives and visuals such as graphs to teach mathematics.

As we use mathematics all the time in our world, parents are in an ideal position to show their daughters this link. When we go shopping, do banking or cook a recipe, we are using measurement and numbers. Illustrate the relevance of science in their world using real-life scenarios they can relate to. In the film *Legally Blonde*, the character Elle Woods wins her court case by pointing out the witness could not have taken a shower straight after getting a perm or she would have lost all her curls. She cites the complex chemistry involved in creating a perm as evidence.

Improve spatial skills

Girls are generally not as adept as boys at non-verbal problem solving and spatial visualisation. For this reason, make time to help them develop spatial problem solving. This can be achieved by:

- playing puzzles – jigsaws, scrabble, chess
- making pottery and weaving
- making and reading maps
- using physical objects such as blocks to stand for variables in equations
- using physical representations of atoms, electrons, planets
- using examples of diamond and crystal structures in jewellery
- using spatial problem-solving exercises that involve animals.

Ideal day

Teens live in a 24/7 world – switched on, distracted, over-entertained, hyper-connected, revved up and sleep deprived. The idea that there are specific times of the day when people do things best is a foreign concept to most teens. Let's take you through an ideal day.

It's busy just before dawn

It is 3 am and hopefully you are sound asleep. Your body temperature is at its lowest. But even as you snooze, your brain is still 80 per cent activated. It is busy consolidating memories, restocking proteins, repairing cell damage, and strengthening synapses. Soon you will have one of the 200 000 dreams that occur over the course of your life. If you are a woman, you have a greater chance that this dream will be a nightmare. Rapid Eye Movement (REM) or dream sleep is important for memory consolidation.

Not getting enough sleep really makes it hard to have a great day. If you sleep less than 6 hours, it is equivalent to having a 0.05 blood alcohol level. One week of restricted sleep is like 24 hours of consecutive wakefulness (or having consumed ten beers). Sleep loss impairs the

> Sleep loss means you age faster and gain weight.

body's ability to regulate blood sugar, which means you age faster. It also helps you gain weight.

With all that going on it's no coincidence that between 3 and 4 am is the peak time for night-work errors, for auto and truck crashes and gastric ulcer crises.

Up, up and away!

Have teens rise at about 7 am on week days. Waking up causes violent increases in heart rate and blood pressure and a peak in levels of cortisol, so start the day as gradually as possible. The first half hour after waking, your performance is woeful, so this is not the time to make major decisions or to hold important conversations.

The two rush hours of the day (getting out of the door in the morning and getting to bed at night) probably cause more daily angst in most households than any other issue.

At these times, habits and routines are your friends and random chaos and spontaneity are your enemies. Ideally, we would have instilled these into our teens from a young age but parenting tricky teens can be, well, tricky. Nevertheless, it is possible to teach slightly older dogs new tricks.

With the morning rush hour, we need to work backwards from the end result in steps to the beginning, breaking it down into sub-tasks. We start building responsibility for the end task and then work slowly back through the entire sequence.

1   In car with bag packed dressed for school by 8.20.

2   Bag packed 8.10.

3   Lunch made and packed 7.55.

4   Teeth brushed, hair combed 7.40.

5   Breakfast eaten 7.15.

6   In shower 7.10.

7   Waking up by 7.

> It is possible to teach slightly older dogs new tricks.

Start by training your teen to be in the car by 8.20 am. You may have to do everything else in order to get them there. Try to get this happening consistently for a few weeks. Then start moving backwards by having them pack their school bag under your supervision, then without being supervised. After a few successful weeks, introduce making your own lunch. Be patient. These changes in morning habits will take a while but there will be moments of progress.

Breakfast

Breakfast should be high-protein, low carbohydrate to kick-start mood and concentration. A good example is a protein shake smoothie with berries, an omelette and a glass of milk. Avoid fruit juices and muffins and stay well away from energy drinks. Teens might consider taking a good quality multivitamin and at least 1000 mg of fish or krill oil.

If your teen drinks coffee, now is a good time to have one of their two daily coffees. Caffeine binds with the receptors

Don't forget a water bottle.

for adenosine, a natural chemical important in wakefulness. Ideally, replace coffee with green tea during the day. Pack some water, the remaining smoothie, a few handfuls of almonds and a protein and salad roll for your teen to take for lunch. Don't forget the water bottle. Your teen's brain needs to be hydrated.

Early morning

It's time to focus. Young people are easily bothered by distractions in the early morning, much more so than in the afternoon. The advice is to lessen distractions and not to multi-task at this time. When we try to do two things at once, neither gets completed or learned. Multi-tasking means it takes 50 per cent longer to do things. Talking on a mobile phone while driving increases the risk of crash by 1.3 times. Texting triples the risk.

Increase the amount of incidental exercise your teen has in a day. Take the stairs. Going down stairs is like an energetic walk; going up is equivalent to running. Moderate exercise makes us feel less tired. Between two and a half to four hours after you wake up, attention peaks. It's best to use this time for the information you really need to learn. Restrict peak hours for focused attention tasks. Around 11 am is the peak learning time for the day for most teenagers. Late morning is also the best time to learn new motor skills.

Lunchtime

Lunch is ideally the major meal of the day. It's good to sit quietly for five minutes after you finish eating and then walk for fifteen minutes. Try to keep the time your teen eats fairly regular as food intake sets internal body clocks. Just by living, you burn between 50 and 70 per cent of the energy you consume – 20 per cent goes to the brain, 10 per cent to the heart and kidneys, 20 per cent to the liver, and up to 10 per cent for digestion.

Early afternoon

Lots of teens have a down time around 2.30–3.30 in the afternoon when they make more mistakes and learn least well. This is not a great time for taking in new information or talking through relationship issues. If they do have to take in details, moving around while doing it or taking notes might help. During the afternoon, it's good to have snacks such as almonds and apples to lift mood and energy. Teens are like locusts: they arrive with a ravenous appetite and need to refuel when they get home.

When picking up school students, please be careful as 3.30–4.30 is a time when single vehicle accidents are common (as they are around 2–4 am). Blood pressure runs higher in the afternoon, but it is not a bad time to go to the dentist. Anaesthesia for dentistry lasts three times as long as the same amount given in the morning.

Late afternoon

This is the best time for physical activity. Your body is generally at its best now. For body-conscious teens, exercise at this time may result in 20 per cent more muscle strength than in the morning. The heart works more efficiently, reaction time is at its peak, as is core body temperature. Most sports records are set between 3 and 8 pm. Liver function is at its best between 5 and 6 pm.

> Have some quiet or meditation time twenty minutes before dinner.

Evening

Have some quiet or meditation time twenty minutes before dinner. Dinner should be lighter than lunch and at least three hours before your bedtime. It takes about 50 per cent longer for the stomach to empty dinner than lunch. Sit quietly for five minutes after you finish eating then walk for fifteen minutes.

Homework is often better completed in sprints of about twenty minutes' duration rather than slogging through a marathon. Despite what some teens think, homework doesn't achieve its purpose when it's completed by the parent.

Some teens feel fresh and able to complete all of their school tasks before dinner, while others need to roam free and shake off the day before completing homework. Discuss this with your teen and plan with them when the ideal time to complete school tasks is every day. However, they only get computer time once the homework is completed.

About 9.30 pm commence the wind-down for the day. Soak in a warm bath. An hour or so before bed lower the lights – use lamps, sip herbal tea, create to-do lists for tomorrow. Consider using the information in the issue on computer addiction to restrict access to the internet. Melatonin starts to increase in the evening. If your teen is learning new information they might listen to a tape or podcast of key information, for about twenty minutes.

Have your teen to bed ideally by 10.30 pm. Don't allow them to watch TV, use the computer or work in bed. Remember the sleep cycle occurs every 90–120 minutes. Try to help your teen catch it.

Motivation

Motivating that slumbering, seemingly immovable, object known as 'teenus minimalus' can be an ordeal for any parent. Children, who were like roosters as little kids, up at dawn and making one hell of a din, reach their teen years and appear to enter semi-retirement. Lazing about on couches, sleeping through half the day and lolling about. A coherent conversation seems beyond them, despite always being able to muster enough energy to post on Facebook.

Some teens seem so low in motivation, parents don't know whether to become a screeching banshee or enrol in a course with a motivational guru on the art of pep talks. Cleaning up bedrooms, picking up after themselves and helping around the house are issues for many parents, but the main motivational issue is schoolwork and homework.

> Motivation has more to do with overcoming fears than anything else.

What lurks behind the doldrums

The most important thing to know is that not feeling motivated hasn't really got much to do with motivation. It has more to do with feeling anxious and worried. This is the formula:

Fear + Worry + low levels of dopamine = loss of motivation

Motivation has more to do with overcoming fears than anything else. It feels much easier to not put in some effort than to risk failing at something. Fears loom larger if we try to avoid them. Teens who are under-achieving at school may be focusing on being accepted by their friends to the detriment of their academic success. 'It's cool to be a fool' is a motto that doesn't get you very far in life.

Avoiding fears and worries is addictive stuff. Teens aren't known as long-term thinkers so the short-term pay-off of mucking around with your friends to avoid boring schoolwork that they feel they are likely to fail at anyway is intoxicating. The problem is that as the peer group matures, they become less tolerant of clownish, distracting behaviour and eventually shun teens who act this way. Unfortunately, this compounds the problem for the unmotivated teen. Not only do they fear failure or being exposed as stupid in school, they begin to feel isolated and unpopular as well.

News flash! Some teens hate school

Most teens grudgingly like school, feel successful there and find it a good place to hang out. They describe most of their teachers as 'not bad' or 'all right', which is high praise in teen terms! But there is another group of teens who can't stand school. They regard it as a misery inducing form of juvenile detention. In this they share the viewpoint of a surprising number of very successful people. However, those successful people were usually able to continue their education to the point that they could succeed.

Parents shouldn't try to get unmotivated teens to like school. That's not going to happen any time soon. The point is to get them to do enough school in order to succeed in a career.

Homework

It's hardly an earth-shattering statement but teens who don't like school hate doing homework. Homework has the capacity to drive a nail of conflict through the hearts of families. Homework is worth doing, but not if it is creating pain in the family or even worse, is mainly being completed by the parent. That just makes the problem worse.

I sometimes suggest that parents write to their teens' school saying, 'At the moment my teen and I are going through a rough patch. While I am hopeful that this will pass, one of the points of conflict is the completion of homework. While I want my child to succeed in life, the battles over homework are not being constructive. I want you to know that I am supportive of the school and am appreciative of the help that you give my teen. I am also supportive of consequences you may put in place should my teen not complete homework. At this time, however, I am unable to supervise or control the completion of homework.'

Homework, independent work and practice are helpful for teens but your job is to be a parent. Parenting an unmotivated teen is tricky enough; you don't need additional jobs.

> If you think you can offer a bribe big enough for your teen to really try to do well, use it.

Does bribery work? If you read any of the texts on motivation they will tell you that doing something for its own sake is more powerfully motivating than having an inducement or a reward. Trouble is, some tricky teens are not interested in anything at school and if you waited for them to find an interesting angle to their studies you would be waiting several lifetimes. For this reason, if you think you can offer a bribe big enough for your teen to really try to do well, use it. There's nothing really wrong with extrinsic rewards such as money, holidays and freedom. How many people would still go to work if they weren't being paid?

However, rewards seem to lessen the motivation for doing a task for its own sake. So if you are going to go down the path of bribery, be aware that you will need to keep putting your hand in your pocket until they complete school. Let's discuss some powerful techniques parents have used to motivate their teens at school.

Set small goals and one large one   For each subject at school, ask your teen to set a small goal each week and to write it down. A goal might be to read and understand one chapter of a set book. When they have achieved that goal, give it a tick (or points towards a reward if necessary). Ask your teen to nominate their favourite (or least hated) subject at school and identify it as the one they will 'go for broke in'. In this subject, their aim is to top the class. This is the subject that they will use to judge themselves by.

Get them organised   If your teen is completing the senior years of school, disable their Facebook page until after the exams. With really disorganised, unmotivated teens, there may be no alternative to pitching in yourself. Help them to get up to date. If they have fallen behind in any subject, have a working bee to catch up. Request that they ask teachers to help by saying something like, 'I lost motivation for a while in this subject but now I'd really like to catch up.'

> It is remarkable how motivated you can feel when you have a tidy space to study in.

If they haven't been in the practice of taking notes, get them to start. If they have become embarrassed about asking questions in class, set a goal of having them ask one question per class. If that is too embarrassing, ask the teacher after class. If they've missed notes, ask for copies of them. Help them to write a revision summary for the subject to date topic by topic. This can be a mind map or a flow chart that links the entire topic of learning together. If their study area has become a mess, clean it up. If they won't clean it, you can. It is remarkable how motivated you can feel when you have a tidy space to study in.

Some unmotivated teens feel overwhelmed and disheartened. They no longer think there is anything they can do to succeed at school. Use post-it notes to help them see each of the steps towards a successful outcome. On the first post-it note, write the successful outcome for that subject. On another post-it note, write the step before that and on another, the step before that. Now add the first step you could take. You wouldn't enter a marathon without doing a series of shorter training runs first and the same thing applies to doing well at school. Regaining motivation is a step-by-step process.

Help your teen give up believing that they know how smart they are

Most teens who feel unmotivated think everyone else knows more, is more talented, is smarter and has more brains. My research shows that most students have absolutely no idea how well they are going to do at school. It is highly likely that they are more intelligent than they realise. It is also highly likely that most of the people around your teen in class are not quite as clever as they appear to be. Remind your teen of this.

Build on their strengths and forget about their weaknesses

Encourage your teen to notice their strengths. Highlight them yourself. Success in life is about doing more of what you are good at and less of the things you are not good at. Serena Williams is not known because she can do mathematics. Einstein wasn't known because he played soccer. When you focus on the things you find more enjoyable and interesting at school, even the things you find harder become easier.

Help them use their time in school well

Many people muck around in school and then wonder why they have to do so much work outside of school. Consider asking your teen to sit towards the front in class. If they can focus and listen well while at school they can save themselves endless hours. This is valuable time saved that they can use for hanging out with friends and having fun.

Be honest

If your teen has felt unmotivated, they may have done anything to avoid doing their study. The world is full of excuses: 'The dog needs a walk,' 'I have to finish this game and then I'll study,' 'I'll have a nap and study when I wake up.' You have to be tough enough to insist that the work is done *before* you do the computer games/TV watching/chat-room messaging etc. Do a deal in this area with your teen.

Help them to be honest enough to admit that lying in bed, with the computer on, listening to music, with a DVD in the background and messenger open to chat with friends, is not and will never be, studying. Have some study time sitting at a desk or table with *no* electronic distractions.

> Consider asking your teen to sit towards the front in class.

Change of routine

If your teen has been finding it difficult to get motivated, suggest they change their study pattern. For example, they might study in a local library rather than at home, or switch study rooms. Just as you learn to surf best by surfing, teens learn to succeed in exams and essays by giving their undivided attention to study. That means practising in the same conditions that they will be performing in. There won't be electronics or music in the exam room!

Why should you care?

Teens might be able to dismiss all of the above points by saying, 'I can't do it,' or 'I can't be bothered,' or 'This sucks.' That is just the part of them that is scared, talking them out of it. The scared part thinks that if they try and fail, it will be much worse than never having tried in the first place.

Suggest they think about what would happen if you applied this thinking to the whole of your life. You wouldn't learn music and start a band because U2, Pink and 50 Cent have already done it. You wouldn't talk to someone you like because they could reject you. You wouldn't go out, because it would probably disappoint. You wouldn't live the life you could live because you would lack the daring and courage.

There are eight billion people on this planet, don't let one ruin your day

You know the number one fear of all time? Death? No. Speaking in public? No. The number one fear is that other people will think badly of you. And you know what the biggest and saddest joke about that fear is? Most people don't think about you at all.

Most people are so busy or so self-absorbed that they haven't got the interest or the energy to judge you.

There's a chance that your teen could throw away a really successful, enjoyable life by worrying about something that doesn't even exist. It's up to them. But what other people might think of them if they stuff up is no reason to give up on themselves.

Perfectionism

The moment of victory is much too short to live for that and for nothing else.

Martina Navratilova, Champion tennis player

I am partial to a degree of perfectionism in airline pilots, surgeons, dentists and bridge builders. No-one wants these people to take a near-enough-is-good-enough approach to their work. And yet, perfectionism is a form of self-torture that can lower performance at critical moments. Perfectionism is anxiety that thrives in fiercely competitive environments. While it can lead to striving for success, it can also lower accomplishments, creativity and performance. Like many attributes, perfectionism runs in families.

There is a simple probability rule: it is much more likely for things not to go exactly to plan than it is for them to be exactly as you expect. It is more likely for things to be in the wrong place than in the right one, for mistakes to occur on the road to success, for there to be different ways of achieving success rather than one single pathway. The brutal outcome of this probability rule is that unreformed perfectionists are condemned to lives of stress, disappointment and dissatisfaction. Teens who try to control the world are bound for torment.

Paradoxically, the sense of not being able to control events or outcomes can lead teens to strive for perfection. This is like racing to find the end of a rainbow. Consequences of perfectionism include being rigid, anxious and unspontaneous, becoming a workaholic or over-cautious, developing body-image problems and not trying out new things.

> Perfectionism runs in families.

Your teen may be a perfectionist if they:

- worry about mistakes and don't give themselves credit for their successes

- can't enjoy their achievements because of other possible failures

- are harshly self-critical when they make a mistake

- become incredibly dramatic over the smallest mistake

- get upset unless things are 'just so'

- frequently criticise and find fault in others (especially parents!)

- have extremely high standards

- sometimes seem rigid and inflexible in their problem-solving

- are fussy about their appearance or possessions

- can't get started on work until they have the answer.

High achievers and perfectionists

We can be misled into thinking that perfectionists are just brainiacs with all the willpower in the world and the determination to succeed at all costs. The truth is that perfectionism can lower performance and sabotage success. Some perfectionists can be successful, but attaining that success involves many of them flogging themselves into an exhausted wreck of a life.

Perfectionists and high achievers both set high goals and work hard towards them. However, a high achiever can be satisfied with doing a great job and achieving excellence, even if their very high goals aren't completely met. Perfectionists will accept nothing less than, well, perfection. 'Almost perfect' is seen as failure.

Perfectionists focus fiercely on a single result. Their determination is admirable, but they can be so focused on the result that they tense up and choke as they approach significant milestones. High achievers, by contrast, focus on the way they get to a result. They put more focus on the process of getting there than the end point. High achievers also want good outcomes but because their focus is on the way they perform rather than the outcome of their performance, they are less likely to choke when the stakes are high.

Looking for flaws

It's a very rare day for a perfectionist when everything is completely right. They are intolerant of flaws in themselves, their parents, siblings and school. The disdain they express at others' imperfections conceals anxiety about their own flaws. This is not a recipe for a happy life. Nor is it a pathway for success. It's a recipe for caution, hesitation and avoidance. Success usually entails focusing on and building our areas of strength, while not being too perturbed by our areas of vulnerability.

> It is a very rare day for a perfectionist when everything is right.

The only perfectionist in the house?

Perfectionism seems to run in families. If your teen cannot abide making mistakes, coming second or getting a lower than expected result, have a good look around the family. Who else is fiercely competitive and speaks derisively about coming second best? We all need to be mindful of the wisdom of Khalil Gibran.

> *Your children and not your children.*
> *They are the sons and daughters of Life's longing for itself.*
> *They come through you but not from you*
> *And though they are with you yet they belong not to you.*
> *You may give them your love but not your thoughts,*
> *For they have their own thoughts.*
> *You may house their bodies but not their souls,*
> *For their souls dwell in the house of tomorrow,*
> *   which you cannot visit, not even in your dreams.*
> *You may strive to be like them, but seek not to make them*
> *   like you.*
> *For life goes not backward nor tarries with yesterday.*

Khalil Gibran *The Prophet*, 1923.

Helping perfectionist teens

Perfectionists can be difficult to change. They may see their perfectionism as the reason for their success so far. Usually out of all proportion, they fear that mistakes will be disastrous. Perfectionist teens are high on catastrophising and low on self-forgiveness. Shifting them will be a gradual process. Some ideas on how to do this are outlined below.

No expectations, no disappointments   To be a perfectionist, you need to be clear minded – so clear minded, in fact, that you feel like you have the power to predict the future and the will-power to always make it happen that way. Most teens need to build their ability to plan and predict. It's the reverse for perfectionists. Parents can help by suggesting they don't predict too far in advance. Anticipating school marks or who will come first distracts from the task of preparation. It also robs teens of the joy of life.

Parents of teens need to help them focus on the present. While a perfectionist teen's mind leaps and runs ahead, anticipating obstacles, parents need to guide their focus back to two things:

- What are you doing right now?

- What's your immediate next step?

When parents do this, perfectionist teens will raise some future contingency and threat. Don't be swayed by this. Just repeat the two questions above and say, 'When you can answer those two questions, get back to me.' On their return, repeat the same questions. It takes time and patience to guide a perfectionist back to the present but it may be one of the best gifts a parent can give their teen – a chance at a happy life.

Coaching in mindfulness   Timothy Gallwey wrote a series of books that I heartily recommend to parents of perfectionists – *The Inner Game of Tennis, The Inner Game of Music, The Inner Game of Golf* and *The Inner Game of Work.* Of these I prefer *The Inner Game of Tennis.* Gallwey revolutionised professional tennis coaching. He noticed that when he gave a clear instruction such as, 'I want you to hit the ball into the left corner of the tennis court,' the performance of players worsened. The coaching was inadvertently activating the critical or perfectionistic part of the self. Instead of the player putting all their energy into hitting the ball, the perfectionist part was worrying and getting distracted by thinking, 'Is that far enough left?' 'Should it be further back?'

> It takes time and patience to guide a perfectionist back to the present.

This led Gallwey to alter his coaching methods to a mindful approach. This involved the player first learning specific sub-skills (backhand, forehand serve, volley). Then Gallwey would say something like, 'Don't worry about where the ball goes, right now all I want you to do is to focus on just this bit of the skill, be present and aware of it, try to focus on just doing this bit as flawlessly as possible.' When players were able to give their full awareness to the skill they were using right then, their performance improved.

Helping perfectionist teens break tasks into sub-skills and then focusing on completing them as mindfully and as flawlessly as possible will improve their performance. You can help teens see that anticipation is a form of distraction that interferes with doing things well. Teach them to be here now!

For example, a teenage daughter is worrying about the mark she will achieve on a final year exam. As a parent, you could:

a) join her in panicking about the mark

b) try to soothe and reassure

c) try to shift her focus.

Soothing and reassurance are admirable but rarely successful as an initial manoeuvre. Trying to soothe a perfectionist teen too quickly can firm their resolve to panic. Instead, be determined and single-minded in shifting their focus to the immediate task ahead. Some perfectionist teens become so frazzled and wired on adrenaline that they will work long into the night on a school project. Remember, you are the one with the fully functioning frontal lobes. It's fine to be the bossy parent and to instruct them to stop working and go to bed, but you'll need to make time to help them the next morning.

The art of erratic parenting

Perfectionist teens often like to control family life. The uproar and upset that ensues when things don't go the way that they want allows them to stealthily take control of family events. Spontaneity has leached out of the family. To their immense annoyance, you need to regain some of the quirky, unpredictable and erratic parts of family life. They won't love you for it, but it is important that they learn they don't control the world. Do things at odd times. Arrive when you weren't expected and depart suddenly. Dance, play music, take them on outings without telling them the destination in advance. Push the boundaries of playfulness.

Do things with your teens that they've never done before. Quirky adventures don't have to take a lot of time or money, but they do take thought and planning. Go somewhere they've never been before or do something new. Don't settle for anything less than an interesting life.

If you're scared of getting things wrong, you won't try new things. If you don't try new things, you become bored and boring. A risk for perfectionists is that life becomes mundane, dull and routine. Some perfectionist teens think if they get things right, there will always be a big reward. These teens may become passive good girls and boys who turn into compliant and often bitterly disappointed adults.

> Push the boundaries of playfulness.

Never let them control the kitchen

Some perfectionists are lovely helpful teens who will take on household duties for you. They may even do some things better than you do them yourself. But don't let them take over the cooking. As delightful as it is to have your teen cook for you, perfectionists can approach cooking like a head chef. Sometimes the teen stops eating meals with their parents, claiming to have eaten while preparing the meal. Eventually, you have a thinner and thinner teen on your hands and suddenly the connection between perfectionism and body shape hits and you have an eating disorder to deal with.

A short course in humility

Most perfectionists don't have a great sense of humour. The world isn't full of jokes when you have to win at all costs. As perfectionist teens focus on being better than everyone else,

> Appreciation is the antidote to perfectionism.

they are not always the most humble of souls. Parents can help them to have a generosity of spirit. Increase the amount of gratitude expressed in the family. Talk about the strengths of people and the variety of ways they contribute to the world. Praise people more heartily and help your teen look for the best in others. Appreciation is the antidote to perfectionism.

Pessimism

Henry Ford was correct when he said, 'Whether you think you can or that you can't, you are usually right.' Developing a positive mindset where teens can improve over time and overcome setbacks is a powerful predictor of success. Here are some ways that parents can shift teens from 'can't do' to 'can do'.

Fall down seven times, get up eight

We all have setbacks. There are times when we have to pick ourselves up, dust ourselves off and start again. Most of us are experts in this because this is the way we learned to walk. Sucking at something the first few times you do it is the first step to getting good at it.

Praise effort more than ability

Tell your kids that they are geniuses, but they don't know it yet. It's good to know that your parents think you are wonderful.

Then focus most of your comments on effort. 'You really worked hard at that. Well done!' 'I noticed you really tried your best at that, I'm impressed!' or 'Wow, your practice seems to be really paying off.'

Mistakes are opportunities to learn

If a teen thinks they didn't do well at something because they lack intelligence, they give up. When they can see they are on a pathway of improvement, they persist. Mistakes are an essential part of learning. The physicist Niels Bohr defines an expert as 'a person who has made all the mistakes that can be made in a very narrow field.' Parents can help teens learn that when you make a mistake all it means is that you haven't learned how to get it right yet. Creating something new involves making lots of mistakes. One example is the bestselling Dyson vacuum cleaner. The inventor, James Dyson, made 5127 prototypes of the vacuum before getting it right. 'There were 5126 failures. But I learned from each one. That's how I came up with a solution. So I don't mind failure.'

> Sucking at something the first few times you do it is the first step to getting good at it.

Shark thoughts and dolphin thoughts

We have thoughts flying through our heads all the time. Some of those thoughts are sheer genius. Others should be taken out the back and quietly strangled. It is a day of enlightenment for all of us when we realise that not all of our thoughts are equally

> Not all of our thoughts are equally valuable.

valuable. Teens don't know this. They tend to believe all their thoughts are brilliant.

For this reason, it is useful to introduce into family life the idea that there are two types of thoughts: shark thoughts and dolphin thoughts. Shark thoughts are the negative ideas that circle around and eat up our confidence and optimism. Dolphin thoughts are more positive and helpful. When a pessimistic teen starts expressing a lot of shark thoughts, it can be useful to pick them up and say something like, 'OK I've just heard ten shark thoughts in a row, now let's hear a few dolphins.' It will take a while for a teen to learn the difference between shark and dolphin thoughts but you've got time.

Let's give you a few example shark and dolphin thoughts.

Example shark thought	Possible dolphin alternative
I'm no good with numbers	That's why they invented the calculator
I'm no good at languages	I haven't taken the time to learn a foreign language
I'm not good at singing	I don't care about being a good singer
I'm not good at drawing	I'm going to take an art class and learn to draw
I'm not at the top of my class	For the careers I'm interested in, I don't really need to have the highest marks

Dealing with setbacks

No-one enjoys making mistakes, but if we don't learn from them, we're destined to repeat them. It's hard to keep your enthusiasm up when you weren't selected for a drama part or a sports team or you failed a test.

Parents can help teens to analyse mistakes. After a setback, you could ask:

- OK, so you didn't do as well as you would have liked. What can you learn from this?

- What parts of it did you do well?

- What parts of it didn't go as well as you had hoped? How much work would be involved in getting better at those parts?

- Would you change the way you prepared for it next time? In what ways?

- I know you can do better at this if you want to. Do you want to try again?

- How can I help you with this?

If they decide not to have another go say, 'OK, but don't let your decision trick you into believing that you couldn't get better if you tried.'

Turn losses into tournaments

You may have already done this as a kid. After losing at a game, you may have said, 'Best out of three is the champion.' If you didn't win that tournament, perhaps you may have said, 'Best out of five is ruler of the universe.' Teach your kids that there is no loss; there's always a chance to have another go.

'I noticed' feedback

Parents can use 'I noticed' feedback for positive and negative behaviour. The number of comments made to teens that begin with the phrase, 'I noticed', shape behaviour powerfully:

- I noticed you like to draw.

- I noticed you are really trying hard.

- I noticed you're reading a good book.

Believe me, they will notice that you noticed!

Parents can also calmly draw attention to negative behaviour: 'I notice you are up when you are supposed to be asleep,' or 'I notice that you are feeling upset right now.' This gives kids a chance to explain their actions or comply with their parents' wishes. For more on using this type of feedback, see the section on communication on page 75.

There is no try!

As Yoda the Jedi master puts it, 'Do or do not. There is no try.' Parents shouldn't accept 'try' either. When kids say they are going to try, ask them, 'Does that mean you are going to do it or not?'

Focus on process, not result

Successful sports teams play the game the same way regardless of the score in the game. Focusing on the result causes people to panic or freeze up. Parents' comments can cause a shift in their child's awareness. Instead of commenting on the result, find something you like and notice it. For example, 'You sang the first few bars of that song beautifully. It's coming together.' Avoid the temptation to then add suggestions of ways to improve.

Role models

Young people today lack positive role models. The media seems determined to serve up kids role models of testosterone-fuelled bozos or ditzy socialite women. The idea that you can partly shape your life on an admirable person is alien to some teens. Talk about the people you admired as a kid. Explain why they have been important. Talk about the everyday heroes who have inspired you.

'Do or don't do. There is no try.'

Think of a time when it was hard

We've all done things that at first seemed impossible. We've all struggled. Share some of those stories with your teens so they know that you have shared the same doubts as they have. Talk about times when you could have given up but you didn't.

Talk about successes

Teens want their parents' approval. The way you provide praise will shape their future efforts. Let them know you are proud of them. Try to include in your delight at their success a comment on the effort that went into their success.

- I am so proud of you for getting that A, I know how much work you put into that project.

- You were great today. All that practice has really paid off. I'm proud of you.

- Wow, when you put your mind towards something, you really work hard and get it. That's great.

Be exuberant

If you become the proud parent, teens will say you're embarrassing them. Don't believe them. Maybe don't do it in front of other people, but in private, let them know that you love them and think they're fantastic. They may pretend that they hate it but they all secretly lap it up.

Be the antidote to despair

Your teens will become upset at setbacks – they'll label themselves as no good or stupid if they don't get a good mark and they'll compare themselves negatively to others. It is tempting for parents to try to soothe kids out of this or even provide a salutary lesson, 'Well if you'd tried harder you would have done better.' Don't do this!

Focus on effort and improvement. 'I'm sorry you didn't do as well as you'd hoped. If you want to have another go, let's work out a way of getting better at it.' At first, changing your parenting language might feel a bit weird, but focusing on noticing, commenting on effort and emphasising the power of having a go are some of the most powerful ways parents can set kids up for success.

> Focus on effort and improvement will come.

Reclusive teens

Some families have teens who rule the house while the parents retreat to their bedrooms. Others parents rattle about the house while their teen is burrowed deep in their bedroom. This is an increasing trend: teenagers who drop out of the world and drop into their bedrooms. Surrounded by electronic media, they cocoon themselves and rarely venture outside.

Shy and sensitive teens quite often like a bit of alone time, but reclusive teens take this to a new realm. They either give up on school or attend sporadically. Some of them start to live like bats: dangling around snoozing all day and up and fluttering about all night. Broadly speaking, there are three main types of teens who retreat to live in their bedrooms: geeks, freaks and cave dwellers.

Geeks   These are the electronic enthusiasts. They find school dull, unnecessary and irrelevant. These teens ask, 'What can I learn at school that I can't learn from the internet?' They connect with their friends online using online games and social media and feel little need for face-to-face contact. Occasionally, they may get together for role-playing games or play using a LAN (local area network).

Freaks   The world is a threatening place for some teenagers. School for them is full of taunts, bullying, opportunities to fail and feel even weirder. Some of these teens are creative, sensitive people who see themselves as the fringe dwellers of life. On the edge and not fitting into the mainstream, they feel school does not match their artistic sensibilities. These teens are often less socially isolated than the other two groups and can be quite tribal. Lengthy stretches of bedroom occupancy can be interspersed with artistic or musical gatherings.

THE FIRST TEENAGER...

He just grunts & goes back to his cave

Cave dwellers   These teens are the hermits and the escapists who retreat into their bedrooms. Whether it is justified or not, they claim intellectual superiority. School is boring, life is boring, parents are dull and boring. They obstinately and resolutely retreat from the world. Their motto seems to be, 'I don't need a stable relationship, all I need is a secure internet connection.'

A womb with a view

Teens who live in their bedrooms live in world of early retirement: a warm, temperature-controlled, non-threatening place with food and drink on tap and entertainment at their fingertips. Who wouldn't want that? Teens have control in their bedroom. It's the one place where they can determine who they see, who they talk to and what they do without nagging parents. They can play, learn and entertain without being questioned, particularly if they find the outside world or family members uncomfortable. In an ideal world, there would be hubs in schools and communities, like common rooms in schools, where kids can do all of the above and still be in contact with the real world.

Pampered princes and princesses

Prising these teens out of their bedrooms is an interesting process for parents. Of course, you will consider the possibility of anxiety and depression. You'll also no doubt worry about extreme shyness and porn addiction. While these are concerns worth checking, most of these teens are not as unhappy, shy, disconnected or isolated as it first appears. Most are tremendously content in their cocoons.

> The world has little tolerance for hanging out time.

Parents of reclusive teens have tried the rant, the hype-'em-up pep talk designed to rev them into an excited state and inspire them to go to school regularly. The parental walk of despair that follows this is sad to see, but very common. Most reclusive teens are sensitive, caring people. The rev-up talk, designed to increase adrenaline and impress upon them the importance of getting a life and an education, just doesn't work. Often it just increases the teen's sense that the world is a harsh, unpredictable place. Slowly increasing serotonin appears to be the best strategy.

Let them know that you love them and want the best for them. Create connectedness. Link with them online if they agree. Ask them for assistance with computer issues. Watch some of their favourite YouTube clips. Slowly shift these to the rest of the house where you might watch their favourite TV series together.

Expect sporadic shifts back and forth. Periods of involvement may be followed by extended retreats to the bedroom. Don't despair or deliver another useless pep talk. Give them stacks of encouragement to try some different activities in a safe environment. The world has little tolerance for hanging out time and yet this is what parents of these teens need to do. Just hang out.

> Most reclusive teens have sleep disturbance.

If you think they will do it, consider distance education or homeschooling. Gradually encourage more involvement by asking them to do computer research for you, complete projects or computer-based art and extend this to activities like cooking, sport, painting, drama and music. Some reclusive teens are extremely caring towards animals and younger children. Babysitting, volunteering at animal shelters and environmental causes appeal to some.

Most reclusive teens have sleep disturbance. You may have to limit their access to the internet and computer games for extended periods of time each day. Review the suggestions made earlier on computer addiction. As much as you encourage, link to and support them, the day will eventually come when you will have to pull the plug on reclusive teens. Don't expect that day to feature as one of your life's highlights.

Self-harm

Self-harm refers to people deliberately mutilating their own bodies without intending to die. It is different from suicidal behaviour where the intention is to die.

Teens are focused on their bodies and their appearance. Not surprisingly, some teens can also choose to express any distress they feel through their bodies. Even teens who are not distressed are incredibly focused on their bodies. Teenage bodies have become a canvas for expressing individuality. The world seems filled with teenagers taking photos of themselves (selfies) with pursed lips and strange looks. Glamour and celebrity are seen as forms of expression. Tattoos, piercings, tramp stamps, braided or partially shaved hair are all part of the physical way teens demonstrate to the world who they are. These body adornments, while often not to their parents' taste, are not forms of self-harm.

It is not a big leap for teens to use their body to express pain as well as identity. While this is not fun for parents to read about, it's important to understand. Self-harm is always a signal that help is needed. It can be an expression of short-term distress or it can indicate more serious problems. Self-harm may be associated with a variety of emotional and psychiatric disorders including personality disorders (particularly borderline personality disorder), multiple personality disorder, factitious disorder with physical symptoms, psychosis and trichotillomania (hair pulling or twisting).

> Self-harm is one of the most contagious psychological conditions for teenagers.

Self-harm is one of the most contagious psychological conditions for teenagers. Schools and communities experience epidemics of self-harm. These are set off when a high-status teen starts to slash, burn or cut their skin and other teenagers express their distress in similar ways. Whether your self-harming teen is experiencing emotional problems, reacting to stress, has an underlying disorder or is imitating friends, it is advisable to get help.

The 'typical' self-harm syndrome

The most frequent pattern for self-harm is that it begins in adolescence. There are usually multiple episodes of self-harm and multiple types of self-harming behaviours. Usually there is a low risk of death and the behaviour continues over many years. The main emotions associated with self-harm are despair, anxiety and anger.

Understanding common types of self-harm

Self-cutting This includes wrist slashing, carving, slashing and sometimes burning the skin (moonies). Self-cutting is more common among teenage women than young men and is often associated with mood swings, anger, sexual abuse, eating disorders and drug abuse. The usual course is for feelings of anger, self-hatred and depression to increase, leading to intolerable tension. The desire to self-harm is kept secret and the teen seeks privacy.

Teens often appear to be in a flat and unemotional state (like going on automatic pilot) but behind the calm façade, the tension becomes unbearable and is relieved when the person slashes.

The 'automatic pilot' state is important in that it removes the teen from the painful feelings that most of us would experience if we were to try these acts.

Teens can roughly be divided into 'cutters' and 'scratchers'. The act itself may be ritualistic and a common pattern is repeated slashings on the same part of the body in the same setting, stopping when there is enough blood or enough release. However, the sense of release may be followed by feelings of 'badness', depression or disappointment.

The area of the body that is harmed can be significant. It seems that teens who scratch or slash at their arms or legs, while in need of help, may not be as profoundly disturbed as those who harm the central parts of their bodies such as stomachs, chest or genitals. Most harm parts of the body that can be hidden. In an image-conscious world, if a teen harms a part of their body that cannot be concealed easily, it is generally a reason for even more concern.

> The desire to self-harm is kept secret and the teen seeks privacy.

For most, the increase in tension is followed by a release and then pleasure as the blood flows. Humans have a protective mechanism that slows their heart rate when they see their own blood. Self-harming teens use this as a way of soothing themselves. It is effective but destructive.

Self-asphyxiation Choking games where teens deprive themselves of oxygen are another form of self-harm. This sometimes catches on among a group of teens as a way of inducing a numb high through self-strangulation. Reports of this accompanying an erotic high sometimes circulate. Sadly, choking games can lead to death.

Hair pulling   Trichotillomania is a condition in which people pull out tufts of hair usually by twisting hair until it detaches from the scalp. It is often associated with anxiety and it is not uncommon for people with this problem to wear wigs to disguise bald patches. The pain associated with pulling out hair is usually accompanied by a release of tension.

Head banging   This condition is commonly found in people with intellectual disability and usually treated by behavioural programs.

Face picking   This includes scratching or scraping facial skin repetitively and compulsively. It is generally considered to be anxiety based and is often related to poor self-esteem and concerns about appearance. Sometimes teens will compulsively check for pimples and make the condition much worse by squeezing.

Eating disorders   Eating disorders can also be considered as a form of self-harm.

Why do some teens harm themselves?

Self-harm is a hard issue for parents to accept. For most parents, the thought that their teen would want to harm themselves is totally perplexing. It is important to see it as a misguided and self-destructive coping mechanism. There are various reasons that teens self-harm to cope with feelings that overwhelm them.

Ritual, symbolism and religion   Religious purification and atonement through bodily mutilation has been practiced in various cultures for centuries. The Bible refers to tearing out an offending eye and to cutting off an offending hand as it is better than casting the whole being into hell.

Custom or convention   In our culture, ear piercing, leg and bikini-line waxing and circumcision are common practices. Tooth filing in Balinese culture is another example. Societies throughout history have had accepted forms of self-inflicted pain. In this century, the popularity of sado-masochistic sexual practices seems to have been particularly prominent in times of recession. One explanation for this is the internalisation of a confusing and overwhelming external pain.

> Self-harm is a hard issue for parents to accept.

Psychosis   Self-harm can be a response to hearing voices suggesting that the person is bad and should be punished. Some paranoid people believe that mutilating their body in some way may protect them from those who wish them harm.

Regression   Headbanging and body-rocking are common in childhood (head banging is reported in up to 15 per cent of normal young children aged 9–18 months). Teens faced with extreme conflicts may regress to the safety of childhood when satisfaction was mainly achieved through touch.

Rage, frustration and retaliation   Among abused young people, self-mutilation may stem from rage. It's safer to harm yourself than to kill someone else.

Biological conditions   Organic syndromes such as genetic mutation and chromosomal and metabolic aberrations have been linked to self-mutilation. Because painful stimulation has been shown to result in an increased level of endorphins in the bloodstream, self-harm may actually be reinforced by a pleasurable high.

Sexual abuse Teen survivors of childhood sexual abuse or incest may want their parents' attention. Of course, it is not a healthy way to seek attention and it can lead to feelings of guilt, as if the child has brought the abuse on themselves. One way of coping with ongoing abuse is to disassociate yourself from what is happening to your body.

There are three main functions of self-harm.

Aggression The teen feels aggression towards parents and perceives their upbringing as inadequate, controlling or depriving. By self-harming, the teen gains control over their anger by directing it inwards and finding a release for it. Some teens have a sense that it is better to self-mutilate and thereby have some sense of control over the pain they feel than have to cope with (usually emotional) pain imposed by others.

Stimulation Sexual or physical stimulation can return the person to a sense of reality and control.

Self-punishment Atonement for past wishes or acts.

There are differences between self-harm and suicidal behaviours in teens.

SELF-HARM	SUICIDE
More common in young women	Completed suicides are more frequent by young men, but attempts by young women are seven times more frequent

Means differ by gender young women – cutting young men – burning	Means differ by gender young women – overdoses young men – asphyxiation and guns
Low lethality	High lethality
Sense of relief experienced afterwards	No sense of relief afterwards
Repetitious, ritualised pattern	Usually only one or two episodes
Different methods used by the one person	Only one method characteristically used
Seen as 'manipulative' or 'attention seeking'	Seen as serious or as a cry for help
Infrequent death-oriented thoughts	Frequent death-oriented thoughts
Moderate incidence of alcohol/drug abuse	High rate of alcohol/drug abuse

Risk-taking behaviours associated with self-harm

Many behaviours that are not formally considered to be self-harm are risk-taking behaviours that can and often will lead to self-harm. At-risk behaviour often involves the possibility of self-harm but differs in that the sole intent is not to inflict pain.

A behaviour can be considered as 'at risk' if it places the person or others in danger. These include:

- train surfing

- eating disorders

- tranquilliser dependency

- amphetamine ('speed') usage

- repetitive unsafe sexual practices in spite of knowledge and availability of safe sex practices

- repetitively starting fights where the likely outcome is to lose.

The underlying issues in such behaviour are often similar to those faced by young people who self-harm.

To reiterate: the point of this section is not to terrify you. It is to urge you to seek help if you have a teenager who self-harms.

Sexuality and romance

Most parents worry more about teenage sex than teen romances. However, if your teen selects the wrong person to become romantically involved with, it can have dire, long-term consequences. The result of unsafe or unprotected sex can be appalling but the outcomes of entanglement in a disastrous romance can waste years. Whether a teen is straight, gay, bi, transsexual, fetishistic, computer-porn addicted, uncertain or frightened of the whole business, it is romance rather than sex that causes most of the angst.

Gordon Livingstone, in his wonderful book, *How to Love: Who Best to Love and How Best to Love,* comments wisely that deciding who to love has a large role in our life happiness. Let's adapt Gordon's thoughts specifically for teenagers.

The grand swoop of attraction can blind the most sensible of teens. Young love is about as rational as a herd of goats in a fine furniture store. While it's not always possible to put a wise head on young shoulders, a gentle word from a parent highlighting the desirable, or less desirable, characteristics of potential partners can be inestimably valuable.

> The grand swoop of attraction can blind the most sensible of teens.

Teens get swept up in the moment. This is why it is so important for parents to think clearly about relationships. Robin Skynner and John Cleese, in their book *Families and how to survive them,* discussed the concept of 'the screen'. We all have aspects of ourselves that we aren't so fond of. There are parts of ourselves that we'd prefer that the world didn't really get acquainted with. Those parts we put behind 'the screen'. Then we go out and meet people and get attracted to them. But who we desire is not so random. We often find ourselves drawn to people who appear to have strength in an area we feel deficient in.

If I'm anxious and want to be cool, I'll hide my fears and be attracted to someone who appears cool, calm and confident. It may take me some time to discover that the reason they appear to be confident is that they too have placed their insecurities behind their screen. This is why people from violent upbringings can sometimes resolve never to be violent yet find themselves attracted to people who appear calm and peaceful but who have a cranky temper behind the screen.

Who we decide to spend time with, and whom we choose to stay away from, powerfully determines our happiness. In both romances and friendships there is an essential skill in creating satisfying relationships – the capacity to see the world from someone else's point of view. One of my earlier books, *Tricky People*, outlined many types of toxic people who all had one thing in common – the inability or unwillingness to see the world from anyone else's perspective.

It's worth remembering that:

- in any relationship, we are only entitled to receive what we are prepared to give

- the best guide to someone's future behaviour is their past behaviour.

The idea that you can change someone is a very long bet. Teach your teen that someone who acts in a controlling manner early in a relationship is likely to become more controlling.

> Parents ride shotgun for their teens when they are in the crazy madness of early love.

Parents ride shotgun for their teens when they are in the crazy madness of early love. Obviously, this is a subtle business. It is a world of hints, innuendo, considerations and gentle suggestion. There's no point acting like a matchmaker or a divorce lawyer. Parents shouldn't try to prise people out of their teen's lives. Instead, make it comfortable to discuss and provide advice when it is needed. If a teen gets a sense that you are against their choice of romantic partner, they will get angry and defensive. I have seen many teens who have stayed with partners for longer than they should have, just to spite their parents.

Who to nudge your teen away from

Leeches   These vacuums have no life of their own and seem to suck the oxygen out of the air around them. They are emotional vampires.

Drama queens and kings   These teens create relationships that resemble a soap opera. They describe themselves as poetic, passionate, artistic. The rest of the world describes them as pains in the rear end. To be fair, most of us don't show our best relationship cred in our teen years, but if you observe this pattern of high drama over some time, hear the warning bells.

Bullies   Teens who take advantage of vulnerable people. This can be directly belittling and intimidating or neglectfully inconsiderate and hurtful. They could be racists, intellectual snobs or social climbers. Be especially wary of anyone who is cruel to animals. This often indicates an inability to consider life from another's point of view.

Cling-ons and dropkicks   These teens don't so much have a friendship group as a mobile welfare agency. They spend their time rescuing others even when they don't particularly need rescuing. By associating with the needy, they feel reassured, safe and wanted. At first they can appear to be helpful, admirable people. Then you begin to wonder if the lives they want to save are in need of salvation.

Spotlight huggers   These are teens who think they are the centre of the universe. As soon as the focus shifts from them, they do something – anything – to regain attention. Attention grabbers can include elbowing others aside, humour, distraction and even mishaps or accidents. Demands for attention are accompanied by self-absorption. They find sharing the floor with people difficult, listening to them a bother and caring for them a waste of time. Some of these teens are chronically late. This could be just the wayward organisational skill of teenagers, but when it is a pattern, it can be a marker of passive aggression.

Teens with many enemies Remember the best predictor of future behaviour is past behaviour. If you meet a teen with lists of enemies, a series of fraught friendships, and a litany of discarded relationships, firstly assume they have been unfortunate. If you observe that they seem to spend a lot of time discussing the people who have done them wrong, they may be on the road to becoming a hater.

> The best predictor of future behaviour is past behaviour.

Substance abusers Teens who use substances have a tendency to use other people as well. Not all substance-abusing teens are relationship dynamite but if it continues, start to worry. If you think there probably is a problem, there probably is. Someone who fails to take responsibility for their own wellbeing is unlikely to take care of the other people in their life.

Who to help your teen get closer to

Think about yourself when you are at your absolute best in relationships. That's the sort of person you would like your teen to be involved with. Stock the bookshelf with information, safe sex pamphlets and have the birds and the bees talk, but also think long and hard about the sort of person you would really want your teen to love. A happy, balanced relationship is one of the biggest ingredients of a fulfilled life.

You are their biggest role model

The attitudes teens adopt to relationships are drawn from their parents' relationship. Parent who display trust, openness, respect and fun in one another's company show teens how to create wonderful relationships. If you want to give your teen a great gift, treat their other parent really well.

Siblings

The relationship between brothers and sisters contributes greatly to either their parents' emerging insanity or to harmony and happiness. Parenting teenagers is like refereeing a baseball game. Once one sibling has covered a base, the others need to find a different area to cover.

Stereotypically, siblings take on different areas depending on their birth order. Eldest teens often try to be like responsible mini-parents who like to tell people what to do and bring trophies home for their parents to admire. Middle children figure that base one is already covered so they often focus on growing elbows to nudge others aside and become attention-seeking troublemakers. Youngest kids like to laze about, looking cute while trying to get people to do things for them.

Then just when you've got your own family's version of this worked out, one of them goes on a sleep-over and everyone changes bases.

Why they get on each other's nerves

Along with our parents, siblings are the closest genetic relatives we have. We share so many similarities that we magnify differences. This means that idiosyncrasies that we tolerate in non-family members become hot points of contest between siblings.

Differences between children can become chasms when they become teenagers. In the search for identity and independence, siblings can be the kickboard against which teens define themselves. However, the bonds and the loyalty between siblings are strong. A motto that applies to many siblings is, 'I will fight my brother or sister but if anyone fights *them*, look out!'

Siblings and sibling rivalry

To the outside world we all grow up, but not to our brothers and sisters. We remember each other as we used to be. They knew us when we weren't so sophisticated. They know where the skeletons are buried and how to dig them up. Siblings share private family moments and remember family feuds and secrets.

Many people have had the experience of going through a time of enormous personal change, only to go to a family function where their brother or sisters says, 'You haven't changed a bit!'

Given that most parents are managing a group of teens who act like warring baseballers, it's useful to have a bit more perspective on them.

Eldest teens At worst, eldest teens can act like deposed monarchs. Having once tasted the heady world of undivided love and attention, they yearn to return to that idyllic state. 'Ditch the other kids and let's be a happy family again,' could be a request from an eldest. The way many eldest teens resolve this is to be more like their parents. This can lead some of them to be conservative, conforming to family expectations. Some eldests become bossy sergeant-majors, organising games and events and lording it over others. Others take on a semi-parental role caring for the younger children. This can be accompanied by the weight of responsibility, a feeling that everything depends on them if something goes wrong.

Middles   Middle kids are interesting. Their role is in part shaped by the one taken by the eldest. So if the eldest is less responsible the middle can take on all the features outlined above. More typically, the conformity of the eldest allows the middle child to become more radical and provocative. They often become the family jester, comedian, clown, brat, rebel and wild one. Developing a good sense of humour

> Developing a good sense of humour is a common middle child strategy.

is a common middle child strategy. What can't be won through strength or size can be attained through guile and entertainment. If the eldest child has strongly identified with the mother, the middle may become dad's favourite.

Youngests   Youngest teens always know more about eldest teens than eldests know about youngests. They have spent years observing. They learn not to make the same mistakes. Most adoring youngests take their siblings off the pedestal at some point. For them, the older kids hide their vulnerabilities in plain sight. A younger sibling is someone to use as a guinea pig when trying out new tricks and trialling experimental billy-carts. Someone to send on messages. For a while, youngest teens will do anything to emulate the older kids. They think that they are the cutting edge of cool and know the answer to everything worth knowing. Youngests can be the family pet that everyone fusses over and indulges. They can also feel taken advantage of. It is the youngest who is sought out for company when no-one else is available.

Twins   Unlike eldest teens, a twin never has the illusion that he or she is the centre of the universe. Some twins are as intertwined as a tapestry. They share everything. So much so that a special term, idioglossia, is used to describe the jibber-jabber secret language some twins use. New parents get a lot of attention for having twins so similarities can be overly highlighted. Other twins want to be as separate as oil and water. If one likes it, the other hates it. If one twin is good at something, the other can't be. But even in opposition, they remain defined by one another. As they are so similar, small points of difference such as weight, clothing, style and appearance are often sore points. Most parents of twins at some stage have to put the foot down and insist that, 'This place is big enough the both of you!'

> A twin never has the illusion that he or she is the centre of the universe.

Only children   Only children get a lot of bad press. They are often depicted as self-centred egomaniacs with poor social skills and an inability to share.

In reality they are often adept, smart and socially skilled. They often know when to participate and when to disengage and disappear. This skill seems to stay with them throughout life. They are often self-reliant and content in their own company. Perhaps because they are not continually being interrupted by other siblings, they also often have good concentration skills.

Brothers and sisters

Brothers are like enemies who love you. When they are not sharing jokes and pranks they often talk about one another rather than to one another. They can be fiercely competitive trying to outdo the others, but it doesn't take much to have a group of grown-up brothers giggling like schoolboys and laughing their arses off.

> Brothers are like enemies who love you.

Sisters meddle in each other's lives. They can take over the bathroom, steal clothing without a second thought, engage in dramatic huffs, monumental sulks and express disbelief with the slightest flick of an eyebrow and still be as solid as rock.

How to referee

The world of siblings is rich, deeply felt, fiercely fought and hugely protective. They are the people with whom you share the biggest belly laughs and the bitterest of tears. So what are parents to do? You have to realise that you are the prize. All of this activity that goes on is an ongoing match for the Parental Attention Cup.

Sibling relationships are important

Most parents have said to their teens at one time or another, 'You've got to learn to get on with your brother or sister.' They don't have to get along all the time, but having a general sense of goodwill between them helps their ability to mix socially and sensibly in the outside world. Showing that you are serious about them getting on is important. Teens need to resolve differences without physical or verbal aggression and to be able to share, respect each other's and combined property as well as providing comfort and assistance to one another.

Siblings who can't stand each other

All teens say at some point that they hate their brothers or sisters. Some siblings have almost entirely different personalities and interests. Conflict needs to be managed. In families where siblings don't get along, a sense of justice and fairness is essential. Be even-handed and fair. Don't allow it to be a battle of the biggest and strongest wins. Insist on mutual respect. When the going gets really tough, it's all right at times to say: 'This is my house. You both live here and you'll do it my way.'

The way that parents frame conflict is important. Try to explain the source of conflict as distinct from the participants. 'You've both been under so much pressure lately,' rather than, 'He's grouchy and grumpy – you know how he gets.' This lessens the likelihood the siblings will blame each other.

If an altercation becomes violent, protect yourself and the most vulnerable person if you can. Leave the house if you can. Later, it's better to overreact than underreact. Some teens get an intoxicating whiff of power when they become violent. It's crucial that they realise this behaviour is unacceptable. If they won't listen to you, enlist a relative or other adult the teen respects. If the message still isn't getting through, the police are accustomed to speaking to teens to help them change their behaviour. If none of these steps work, seek help from a counsellor.

Pick at random!

In a survey of over 250 000 parents, not one said that they had walked into a room where two teens were fighting or arguing and got it right. Not one parent said their intervention resulted in a teen saying, 'You're absolutely correct, it was me who began the fight in this instance.'

It's OK to work out who started it, remonstrate, send them to their rooms and tell them to grow up or threaten to dock pocket money. It won't have much effect, but please feel free to respond this way. Given that you know you are going to get it wrong, however, every so often consider coming out of left field when resolving an argument between teens. Here's how.

Walk into a room where two teens are arguing and pick at random who was the 'instigator'. Comfort them. Say something like, 'You poor darling, you must be so unhappy to be fighting with your sister. Are you all right?' Then depart the scene. The other sibling will be furious but don't forget you were going to get it wrong anyway. As long as you mix and match over time, no one will be worse off. Most teen acts are highly predictable and when you alter your response, the behaviour often changes. Another benefit is that any expectation that you will play the role of fair referee and problem solver will go completely out the window.

Suicide

The idea that your teen might feel that their life is not worth living is terrifying for most parents. And yet, suicidal thoughts are quite common during the teenage years. In one study by Dr Karen McGraw, 19 per cent of graduating high school students had experienced thoughts of suicide in the past year. Children as young as seven or eight years of age often freak their parents out by declaring, 'I want to die.' Often this has to do with an emerging sense of mortality and a recent death, loss or illness in the extended family.

Having worked with many suicidal teens, my experience is that depression is almost always present, but not sufficient for suicidal thoughts. Teens often go through periods of lowered mood. Many of them have patches of depression. Given that they can be impulsive, it's important to consider why more of them don't think, 'My life doesn't feel worth living. Right. I'm going to go and do something about it.'

For teenagers to want to seriously act on these thoughts, there are usually additional issues that tip the balance: despair and anguish. Despair is a loss of hope. It is a sense of futility about future prospects. Anguish is the feeling of being so trapped by painful events in the past that one can never be freed from them. The teen feels tainted or damaged by the past and that healing can never happen.

Every teen I have seen who has felt suicidal, even those who I later diagnosed with serious psychiatric disorders, were quite logical about their suicidal feelings. They have clear reasons for wanting to die. That doesn't mean that I (or you) should agree with that logic, but it does mean that it is helpful to understand it. Every worried parent wants to know, 'What are the warning signs that my teen might be feeling suicidal?' I wish I could give you a 'tick the box' list but it isn't as straightforward as that.

Three signs to watch for

The first is a change in behaviour. The most obvious is if a usually happy-go-lucky teen isolates themselves in their bedroom, becomes monosyllabic and listens to gloomy songs. It can also work the other way. A teen who appears to carry a black cloud over their shoulders wherever they go suddenly becomes chirpy and bright. You might say surely that would be a good sign. Often it will be, but in some instances it may indicate that a desperate teen has resolved that doing away with themselves is the answer.

> Even if you are worrying about nothing, it is better to act and be sure rather than remain silent and panic inside.

There might be an increase in the use of alcohol, tobacco or drugs. Of the teens who do attempt suicide, many do so after anaesthetising themselves with substances. Any shift in their normal routine can give cause for concern. One young man, prior to attempting suicide, started sleeping in the window seat by the bay window in his home and another started giving away prized possessions.

The second sign to look for is whether the change in your teen's behaviour happens all the time or at certain times. Generally, a change that occurs all the time and in different settings is more concerning. For example, a teen who is gloomy and uncommunicative at home but cheers up when she is with her friends is less worrying that one who appears sad and flat all the time.

The third sign is the parent's level of anxiety. Parents know their teens well. If you are worried, it is time to trust those feelings and act. Even if you are worrying about nothing, it is better to act and be sure rather than remain silent and panic inside.

Asking about suicide

When in doubt, ask. Raising the issue of feelings of suicide is a terrifying business for any parent. *Asking and talking to your teen about this won't increase the risk.* Consider for a moment if it was you who was feeling so desperate. If you faced problems to the extent that you felt the only way out was to die, you would need to find an alternative solution. Whatever the solution might look like, it would begin with talking about it.

One way of asking is to say, 'You've seemed miserable lately and I am worried about you. Can you tell me a bit about what is happening for you?' If they are evasive, you may need to be more direct. 'I've been worrying that you've been so sad that you've felt like your life isn't worth living. Is that so?' If they deny that this is the case you might say, 'Well, I'm still worried. Can you reassure me a bit that I shouldn't be so worried about you?'

If they admit that they have been feeling suicidal, you might say, 'I think we need to see someone to help you to feel better about your life. I'll find out who would be best. Do you feel that you can keep yourself safe for a few days while I find the right person?' If they say they can keep themselves safe, say 'Promise?' Secure a firm promise from them and ask them to tell you if that feeling changes.

If your teen feels unable to keep themselves safe, it is time to either contact a crisis service, attend a session with your general practitioner or go to the emergency department of your local hospital. Get help now. Treatment makes a difference.

Twentysomethings

Pull your pants up,
Take your hat off,
And get a job

P.J. O'Rourke

Coming home from a hard day at work to find a twentysomething lounging on the couch, eating the last of the crackers and dips and watching a marathon re-run of *The Simpsons* episodes would try the patience of a saint. Huff and puff all you want, but it will only be your own teeth that will be grinding.

Some families get lucky and their 16-year-old teen is clear about their direction in life. Other families have teens who bumble about a bit into their twenties but manage to find themselves. A third group of teens, however, stumble about trying to get a grip on life and only really get there by the skin of their teeth by the end of their twenties. For the parents of these dawdlers, parenting is a test of patience. It is a religious experience, an act of sheer, blind faith. It may be that you have a fledgling adult in the third group.

Working out who you are

Becoming a fully-fledged adult involves working out who you are. This process is called identity formation and twentysomethings have four main ways of going about it.

1. Moratorium   In many ways, this is the healthiest position. It is based around the idea that, 'I'm not quite sure who I am so I'll hang out and wait and see who shows up.' This often accompanies a feeling of contentment and a desire to explore life. All is not so calm in the lives of their parents, however, especially if the young adult decides to remain at home. Parents find themselves asking, 'Are you planning on taking on paid employment at any stage of your existence?'

> Becoming a fully-fledged adult involves working out who you are.

While desperate parents can become frantic and urge their fledgling adult to 'just do something', tolerating uncertainty at this time pays off. Delaying the decision about the type of person you are and becoming aware and exploring how life works sets up a twentysomething for the years ahead. However, parents need to make sure that moratorium doesn't become stagnation. Experimenting and trying things out is exploratory and positive, giving up and becoming vegetative is not. Keep in mind that it takes a few false starts and a few wrong paths before most of us discover a path worth following.

2. *Achievement* These twentysomethings sailed through school collecting awards and accolades as they went. They were adept at gaining social approval. While this is generally positive, some get so hooked on success and praise that it traps them into only doing activities where they succeed. Lucky ones go straight into a career and find it fulfilling. Others miss the positive feedback they got from school and struggle in jobs where they get little recognition for their efforts.

Some fortunate achievers get into their forties before they start to question whether they are living their own life or fulfilling someone else's ambitions for them. Others fall into the black night of their souls at around twenty-seven. The cause is often job loss, relocation or the break-up of a usually long-term relationship. Devastated, these bruised achievers turn to their parents for solace and care. Of course you should look out for your kids in times of trouble, but not for too long. If parents become too accommodating, they may find their wounded achiever relying on them till their mid-thirties.

3. *Confusion* These twentysomethings remain confused and anxious about who they are. They have no idea of their direction in life and add to their anxiety by feeling they should. Their fears and worries make them vulnerable to following fads, cults, role models (both positive and negative) and peer pressure. The strain these twentysomethings place themselves under is enormous.

> The strain these twentysomethings place themselves under is enormous.

4. *Foreclosure* These young people decide that 'this is all I can be' or 'this is all I can expect from life'. Passions that once burnt fiercely, sputter. Dreams are pared back. The shine in their eyes becomes dulled. Without help, many of these people suffer deep despair and disappointment. Some avoid challenges and seek refuge in drugs. It is important to help people in their twenties to choose love and life rather than drugs. Drugs anaesthetise people to life. Foreclosure is the result of not building a life large enough to encompass your dreams.

Parenting the emerging adult

As tempting as it is to throw your hands up in despair, your influence as a parent is not ended when your teen turns twenty. Look at the four main ways to forming identity outlined previously and consider which best describes your twentysomething. Just as we protected our children when they were young, we now need to help them to consolidate as adults. Bear in mind that this is also quite a self-centred time of life. Twentysomethings are focused on making their way in the world. If they are struggling, they become simultaneously more reliant on parents and more disparaging of them. It seems the greatest experts are those with no experience.

How to father a daughter to be a strong woman

Fathering twentysomething daughters is about kind strength. This is true throughout her teenage years, but becomes amplified in importance in her twenties. Girls often marry men who are like their fathers. You want to be the kind of man you want your daughter to choose.

Daughters are most likely to become the shapers of their own destiny when they have their father's respect. This deepens her conviction that she is interesting to and worthy of respect by the men in her life. Fathers can teach daughters how to play the games of the business world, coach them to keep going in spite of feeling anxious, encourage them to achieve rather than to be dependent and to learn that they will not be liked by everyone. A strategy used by girls at school to gain social acceptance is to highlight similarities between people. For example, 'Did you do that? Wow, I did, too. That is so amazing.' In the workplace, however, similarities will not get you far. People get promoted based on their unique capabilities.

Fathers are often the people who can most powerfully show daughters how to blend in with others without hiding what she has to offer. Daughters are notorious for wrapping their fathers around their little fingers. A bit of indulgence is not a bad thing, but don't do things for your children that they can do for themselves. Some daughters admire their fathers so much they consequently view their mothers as dependent, helpless, or hypercritical. These daughters seek power and authority by either becoming like men or becoming liked by men. Here the role of the father is to teach his daughter to value other women.

How to mother a daughter to be a strong woman

Mothering twentysomething daughters is about knowing how good intentions can turn bad. Mothers and daughters talk to each other in ways that are better and worse than other people. They speak more words than daughters and fathers so there are more chances for conflict. It's important for conversations and disputes between mothers and daughters to be direct. Don't hedge about trying to soften the differences too much. For her to emerge as a strong woman in her own right, she has to find points of difference with you.

> Mothers and daughters talk to each other in ways that are better and worse than other people.

Daughters react with annoyance at criticism. Suggestions or questions can come across as a put-down. Mothers should not look to fathers for too much support when this occurs. The mother must show she is strong and can withstand the heat of dispute and the daughter must learn that she can have a strong voice and it will not destroy the relationship.

Daughters in this phase of life often draw mothers in through the sharing of problems. While there is great satisfaction in being sought out for assistance, a common interaction is:

- Daughter brings a problem to share or confide with her mother about.

- Mother makes a few helpful suggestions.

- The suggestions are rebuffed.

- Mother tries to help but becomes frustrated.

- Daughter claims that she has never been understood.

- The emotional intensity increases until both feel upset and misunderstood.

While intensity and involvement are part of the journey, a twentysomething daughter will learn more from the way her mother lives her life than anything she suggests. This is a time to remain connected, but not controlling. A mother who powerfully grasps her own life, who is involved with friends, who takes on careers, projects or social issues and voices her opinions to others demonstrates powerful womanhood to her daughter.

How to father a son to be a strong man

Fathering a twentysomething son to be a strong man is always about respect. Some fathers feel compelled to father as if they were conducting an improvement campaign for their sons. Sons hear these helpful suggestions for improvement as disrespect. A wise father tells his son that he loves him, thinks his ideas and great and then shuts up. No suggested improvements, alterations or hints for different ways of doing things. Nothing else. A son who feels that his father respects him will put in more effort to impress his father than one who feels nothing he can do is worthwhile. Fathers often use teasing as play but sons like it more than daughters. Dad jokes are OK.

Young men of this age don't necessarily want either parent around too much. Drip-feed parenting is sufficient. A few right words go a long way. Fathers who can find an activity that their sons don't mind doing with them can use that to deepen the connection.

Sons desperately want their fathers to be admirable so they in turn can be honourable.

> Be the man that you want your son to be.

This is why twentysomething sons needle their fathers, trying to find or amplify flaws, partly in hope and partly in fear of finding them. A son who sees his father as kind and compassionate, who believes in his kids, has standards and lives with integrity will emulate him. Be the man that you want your son to be.

How to mother a son to be a strong man

A mother doesn't have the battle of differentiation with a son that she has with a daughter. Nevertheless, she needs to tread carefully around setbacks that her son faces. Young men live up to the standard of behaviour that mothers and the women around them demand. Expect your son to treat you well. Do not tolerate being sworn at or disregarded. Insist on courtesy and politeness. Demand that he respect himself and treat people well. If these standards aren't met, remove yourself temporarily, saying, 'I don't have to put up with this.'

Hold high standards for yourself and your son. Tell him that you think he is a good man. Be his biggest supporter. Tell him that he can be a legend. When setbacks occur, be caring but don't try to solve the issue. Some young men want their mothers to solve every problem that comes their way. Bailing your son out of overdue assignments, phoning bosses and making excuses of absences or apologising to others on his behalf thwarts his development into a responsible man. Love him, believe in him and let him face up to the consequences of his actions.

Zombies and zits

Interest in computer games and social media peaks at the same time as most teens are trying to work out their identity. Some teens become so engrossed in a role-playing game or a fantasy series or a specific character that they carry it on in their daily lives. It can be a bit disconcerting for a parent to discover that their teen formerly known as Emma has been 'inhabited' by Zardorth of the third reincarnation. It's understandable to adopt the certainty of a character when you are feeling uncertain about your own place in the world, but parents become concerned that Zardorth may never entirely return to the current time–space continuum.

It's a delightful aspect of teenagers that they can be so imaginatively immersed with multiple identities online and offline. Fear not. Just as perhaps you once suspected a little bit of James Bond or Xena the Warrior Princess lurked within you, their fixation will lessen in time. If it doesn't, the world is full of conventions for people who want to dress up as zombies, Doctor Who and Star Trek characters.

The eruption of a zit is enough to ruin a teen's day. Their chances of romantic links seem to diminish with every bump. Having a parent mildly comment that it is just a zit or pimple and it will go away is not helpful when you're on the cusp of a social catastrophe. Even worse is if a parent takes it as an opportunity to provide a helpful lecture about face washing. Acne is acutely embarrassing. While it's a normal part of these years, if your teen has severe acne it is worth seeking a dermatological appointment to see what can be done.

SECTION THREE

How to change things at home

Creating a new dance with tricky teens

Have you ever watched an old movie and had the sneaking suspicion that you've seen it before? You vaguely remember that the film ends badly. You have a growing recollection that you didn't much like the ending last time. Even so, having come this far, you can't just stop watching. Parenting tricky teens can be like this.

The pattern of battles, arguments and distress with your teen loops endlessly. Parent and teen are caught in a repetitious, useless dance sequence where the behaviours grind on and lead nowhere. The dance causes great drama and sucks the living soul out of most families. It robs everyone involved of their happiness.

> If you are not the person you want to be ... your teen won't be either.

If you relate to this, you've been unhappy for too long. It's time to change things. If you're not being the person you want to be, chances are that your teen isn't either. Since you're the parent in this situation, you're going to have to lead that change. The six-week process that follows has been successfully tried and tested on thousands of families with tricky teens. The point of the six-week process is to jumble up your set family patterns and habits, to give you a new way of thinking that will allow you and your tricky teen to relate in a new way so that you can create a powerfully positive relationship.

The six-week process

Week 1 – Step back a little

Week 2 – Be clear about what you want

Week 3 – Map the dance and go on a treasure hunt

Week 4 – Try out a new dance

Week 5 – Dismantle the old dance

Week 6 – Build a sustainable relationship

The six-week process is not just about removing problem behaviours. It's about creating ongoing, sustainable, positive relationships. Even though the steps are outlined as clearly as possible, you will have to adapt them to fit your own values as a person and your particular tricky teen. While being flexible is desirable, think long and hard before omitting one of the steps. They are there because they work.

You need to be the one with a plan

Teens are short-term thinkers. They act in ways that meet their immediate needs. Their tricky behaviours seem useful because they help them get their own way. To create sustainable change, parents need to think long term about which issues to go to the wall on and which ones to let slide, which values and aspects of a teen's character to encourage and which ones to ignore.

Even with the best plans, parenting sometimes doesn't quite work out the way you hoped. Teens appear to be determined to do things their way rather than the way you would like. Despite the best intentions to improve the quality of your relationship with your teenager, old patterns can linger. This is especially true at times of stress when we all revert to our default and sometimes primitive ways of acting.

Changing the dance with your tricky teen takes time. There will be setbacks. Sometimes everyone falls into despair, feels angry and blames others, which only entrenches problems. At times it will be easy to fall into a pattern of blaming either your teenager or yourself. Tricky family dances can be difficult to budge, but blame is useless. To solve a problem you can't use the thinking that created the problem in the first place. Something new needs to be injected into the relationship for it to improve.

> Try something quirky and unpredictable

Your most inventive parenting won't occur while you're wrapped in a grim battle of wills with your tricky teen.

The counter-balance to the battle is fun. Humour and happiness are great allies in beating problems. Serious problems need to be solved, but they don't necessarily need to be solved seriously. A lovely example of this is the mother who was fed up with her son's swearing. She had tried everything to get him to stop – rewards, star charts, punishment, withdrawal of privileges, stern looks and walking away. She tried the lot.

A week after stopping all her useless strategies, her head cleared. She told her son, 'Every time you use the F word, I'm going to kiss you.' The next Saturday morning, they were shopping together when he uttered the magic word. Without making a comment, she rushed over and planted one of her biggest, motherly smooches on him. Since then, whenever he has even looked like swearing he turns apprehensively to his mother and reconsiders. Sometimes it's the quirky, unpredictable things parents do that break the dance patterns.

Know them better than they know themselves

Before you start the six-week process, you need to know your teen so well that you know what they are going to do before they have thought of doing it. This is not so difficult. Most teens are so driven by habit, neurochemicals, hormones and their reactions to the world around them that they have little idea of what they are going to do next.

You may say that you've known your tricky teen all your life and ask how much more there is to know. The differences between you over recent times have most likely dimmed your vision and blinded you to a few of their good attributes. The aim of compiling a dossier on your teen is to help you to think differently about them.

Their strengths and capacities may have not been seen for a while. It's helpful to bring these to the front of your mind as it will sharpen your plan to change the dance. In the pledge at the start of this book you undertook to watch them with a level of surveillance that most intelligence agencies would envy. Here is your chance to make that a reality.

A profile or dossier of your teen can be constructed using the following categories:

- Values
- Ways of receiving love
- Communication style
- Filters used
- Type of dance you have

Values and priorities

All of us have core values. Linking a change in a dance routine to something your tricky teen already values or is proud of, increases its 'stickiness'. The change is more likely to endure. For example, if a teenager who is a sporadic school attender but also wants to have a financially better life than his or her parents, we will often get much further by discussing ways of becoming rich rather than the inherent value of an education.

Go through the list below and tick the values that your teen strongly exhibits. Then try to identify the five most heartfelt values they have. If possible, both parents should do this separately and then compare lists. It will create a valuable discussion.

- Accomplishment
- Achievement
- Acknowledgement
- Adaptability
- Adventure
- Aggression
- Agility
- Alertness
- Amusement
- Appreciation
- Approval
- Assertiveness
- Beauty
- Being the best
- Belonging
- Bravery
- Calmness
- Caring for children
- Caring for people
- Caring for animals
- Carefulness
- Celebrity
- Challenge
- Charity
- Charm
- Cheerfulness
- Cleanliness
- Comfort
- Compassion
- Competition
- Confidence
- Conformity
- Contribution
- Control

- Conviction
- Coolness
- Cooperation
- Courtesy
- Craftiness
- Creativity
- Curiosity
- Daring
- Decisiveness
- Determination
- Dexterity
- Dignity
- Directness
- Discretion
- Dominance
- Dreaming
- Eagerness
- Ease
- Education
- Elegance
- Energy
- Enjoyment
- Environmentalism
- Excitement
- Extravagance
- Extroversion
- Fairness
- Faith
- Fame
- Family
- Fashion

- Fearlessness
- Fitness
- Freedom
- Friendship
- Fun
- Generosity
- Grace
- Gratitude
- Happiness
- Harmony
- Helpfulness
- Heroism
- Honesty
- Honour
- Hopefulness
- Hygiene
- Imagination
- Independence
- Individuality
- Ingenuity
- Inquisitiveness
- Insightfulness
- Inspiration
- Integrity
- Intelligence
- Intensity
- Introversion
- Intuitiveness
- Inventiveness
- Kindness
- Knowledge

- Leadership
- Learning
- Love
- Loyalty
- Maturity
- Meaning
- Meticulousness
- Modesty
- Money
- Motivation
- Musicianship
- Mysteriousness
- Nature
- Neatness
- Non-conformity
- Obedience
- Open-mindedness
- Organisation
- Originality
- Outdoors
- Outlandishness
- Outrageousness
- Patience
- Passion
- Peace
- Perceptiveness
- Perfection
- Perseverance
- Persistence
- Persuasiveness
- Playfulness

- Pleasure
- Popularity
- Power
- Practicality
- Precision
- Pride
- Privacy
- Reason
- Reasonableness
- Reflection
- Relaxation
- Reputation
- Resourcefulness
- Respect
- Responsibility
- Risk-taking
- Sacrifice
- Satisfaction
- Science
- Security
- Self-control
- Selflessness
- Self-reliance
- Self-respect
- Sensitivity
- Sensuality
- Serenity
- Sexiness
- Sexuality
- Sharing
- Shyness

- Significance
- Silence
- Silliness
- Simplicity
- Sincerity
- Skillfulness
- Solitude
- Spirit
- Spirituality
- Spontaneity
- Stability
- Status
- Strength
- Success
- Support
- Sympathy
- Teaching
- Teamwork
- Thoroughness
- Thoughtfulness
- Thrift

- Thrill-seeking
- Tidiness
- Trust
- Trustworthiness
- Truth
- Understanding
- Uniqueness
- Usefulness
- Variety
- Virtue
- Volunteering
- Warm-heartedness
- Warmth
- Watchfulness
- Willfulness
- Willingness
- Winning
- Wisdom
- Wittiness
- Wonder

Tricky teens can be a conundrum. They may behave abysmally at home and yet hold lofty values. Holding such values is a sign of good parenting. It's also an indication that within them awaits a hero.

When you've devised your list, add it to the tricky teen dossier at the end of the chapter.

The love languages

When battles have been endured for quite a while it's likely that everyone feels unappreciated and disregarded. Increasing the feeling that people are loved in your family is the antidote. You might also like to consider the way your teen receives love best.

Gary Chapman in his book, *The Five Love Languages of Teenagers*, argues that teens function best when parents speak to them in their primary love language. This could be spending time with them, giving them gifts, telling them they are wonderful, hugging them or helping them. Who wouldn't want some attentive quality time, a gift, a bit of praise and physical reassurance from someone who is offering to be at your beck and call? It sounds like paradise. No doubt your teen will be a mix of these. A guide to their personal main love language may be a slight increase in their level of caring for you or their level of relaxation after you have expressed your love in one of these ways.

> Consider the way your teen receives love best.

Quality time Some teens just need time. You don't have to do anything special. Be around, listen to them or do stuff with them. One indication that a teen uses this love language is when they seem settled and happier when you are in the house. They may not seek out long, intense times together, but they like having you nearby.

For them, conversation is good but presence is better. One teenage girl came into my therapy room pale faced and shaken and said, 'My mother read about quality time. Now she keeps wanting to talk to me all the time.' She rolled her eyes and sighed, 'As if I don't have better things to do. I like her nearby, but not in my face.'

Gifts   All teenagers love gifts. For some, a gift is a visible symbol of love. A gift can be much more than just a thing. The best gifts need not be expensive. You don't need to go on a shopping spree to prove you love your teenager. Just buying a special food or drink can be enough. If you buy a lot for your teen and they don't appreciate it, receiving gifts is probably not their primary love language.

Telling them they are wonderful   All teens need to hear you say 'I love you,' 'I'm proud of you,' and 'I think you're wonderful.' Some teens need to hear this more than others. Teens who use this love language are often sensitive to criticism and delighted when praised. Be careful not to turn them into praise junkies. Comments like, 'You're fantastic,' are great to hear but the most powerful comments are about effort – 'It's great you find music so enjoyable. You really practised that piece.' If this resonates with you, make sure to read the issue on belonging and attachment.

Touch   Hug them, pat them, welcome them and kiss them (but don't do it in front of their friends). One indication that your teen uses physical touch as a love language is that you feel like you are raising a gorilla. They wrap you up in hugs, or lean against you or they wrestle their brothers and sisters to the ground. They can leave you alone for days on end and then suddenly are all over you like a rash. If you have a teenage son, you may know that hugging him can be interpreted as being like strangling him. He may be a bit 'touch awkward'. A rub on the shoulder or a quick touch of the arm can go a long way. Touch increases oxytocin, the bonding chemical, and boys need two to three times the amount of touch as girls to get the same response.

Helping   Help your teen with tasks they have to do. Do things for them. Some teens worry about their ability to accomplish things and need your guidance and reassurance. Helping means more than just getting the task done. Suggest that you're ready to pitch in and help organise wardrobes, bedrooms, filing, outlining assignments and projects when they indicate. This is different from swooping and cleaning their bedroom, it is helping them when they're ready to be helped.

Which is your teen's love language? Add it to the tricky teen dossier.

Discovering communication styles

Communication is much more than just using words. Tricky teens have different communication styles. Matching your parenting method to their communication style makes it much more likely that they will consider some of the changes you would like them to make.

Word traders Some tricky teens express almost every thought that flits through their heads. If they have a difference of opinion with you, you'll know all about it. These are the teens who love long discussions, debates

> Communication is much more than just using words.

and disputes. Your home can feel like a courtroom with you being cross-examined by the defence attorney. Getting these teens talking about big ideas and issues rather than knocking heads with you in a battle of wills is a good idea. Some of them are great at telling, but not so great at listening. Be prepared to sit down for the duration and discuss issues. It may take several discussions and a few rambling conversations before major issues are resolved.

Emotional   These kids don't analyse and reply, they feel. Their limbic systems (the emotional processor of the brain) are in control. They pick up on subtle emotional signs and expand them into major dramas. A small, despairing sigh from you can flare up into a display of emotional pyrotechnics. Some can brood silently, steaming with resentment before launching a blistering critique of your inadequacies as a human being. An important thing about these teens is that they express sadness as anger. They launch angry attacks when they feel hurt. The temptation for parents is to reply in kind:

- After all I've done for you!

- How could you say that?

- That's so unfair.

- How dare you!

- How could you be so ungrateful?

Defending yourself is understandable, but with teens, it is never productive. Look behind the words and acknowledge the pain, upset and sadness. Some possible parent responses are:

- Sounds like you are having a horrible day.

- I'm sorry things haven't worked out for you.

- I love you and I understand you are unhappy. When you're ready to solve the problem come and talk to me.

Visual   The majority of teenagers do not learn predominantly through words. We live in the most visual age in history. Teens learn more from watching you than listening to you. Words are largely white noise to them. If they don't see it, they don't believe it. Like it or not, you are your children's major role model. From birth they watch you like a hawk, absorbing every gesture, nuance and saying. Every cigarette, alcoholic drink and swear word, every suppressed argument – they see the lot. If you're having communication issues with a visual tricky teen, you need to change what you do. Show them, demonstrate it, prove it. Trying to convince them or persuade them is a waste of time.

Practical Some teens only understand things by doing them. Experience is their only teacher. You can talk to them until you're blue in the face and it will make no difference. Avoid having long-winded conversations with these teens. Go for the short, sharp bombing raid of ideas. As these teens are so reliant on experience as their teacher, you have a choice. You can get them involved in a broad array of experiences or have them seek out experiences themselves. It is likely these teens will seek out a few experiences that you would rather they didn't anyway.

> Like it or not, you are your children's major role model.

Physical These teens live their lives through their bodies. They respond to comments about appearance, strength, height, beauty, sporting capabilities, musical adeptness, dance skills, fitness and power. You don't have to ask them how they are feeling; they show it through their posture and demeanour. If they're ill or injured, you'll hear all about it. If they start working out and gain muscles, you'll see them. Their skin is their flag. If they are experiencing negative feelings it can be displayed to the world through tattoos, piercings and, sometimes, self-harm. If they are feeling great, they glow, stand straight and look as if they can take on the world.

Your teen is likely to be a mix of these communication styles. Trying to work out their main styles will help sharpen your messages. Your words will have more impact. If communication seems to you to be a major issue in your household, read the section on communication earlier in this book. As with the other attributes, include it in the dossier.

The filters of hearing

Just as light bends through a prism, the same thing can happen to our words. The message received is not always the one that was sent. When a family dance has been going on for a while, it sets up people to hear others' words, intentions and actions in particular ways. Misinterpretations abound.

Consider what typically happens when a kind word from you goes astray. Teens can build up a head of steam that obscures and distorts communication. Let's say you go into their bedroom with the intention of saying, 'Good morning, it's time for school,' and leave labelled as a controlling Nazi who doesn't appreciate the pressures of modern schooling as well as being a time-management control freak.

Your words are heard through a filter of resentment. You are seen as being:

controlling	critical
unloving	selfish

These filters may be extremely unfair. They don't consider your good intentions. The filters are also unconscious. Your teen is not aware that they filter your words in this way. For them, it's an unquestionable truth that you are controlling, unloving, critical or selfish. Here's where you need to cop it on the chin. You may not like it. You won't agree with it but that is how they see and hear you. Your job over the next six weeks is to get around those filters so they can see you clearly. You will be marketing a different you.

Honestly recognising that they hear everything you say through a filter will help you to market your key messages more effectively. You won't sell a lot of toothpaste if you ignore the idea that most people like peppermint. The filters go in the dossier, as well. Think about whether you hear their words through filters, too.

> They hear every thing you say – through a filter.

Your type of dance

Now that we've selected some key values, identified their communication style and the filters they hear you through, it's time to look at the dance itself. Two types of dances occur between parents and teens: see-saws and escalations.

See-saw relationships
Some relationships work like a see-saw – one person is up while the other is down. Rarely are both at an equal level. Some see-saw relationships have an interesting pattern in which one person does all the work to create closeness and intimacy and the other does all the work to mark out distance and autonomy. A parent may phone, text, clean up or do small favours to create warmth in the relationship while a tricky teen sits by impassively or demands their own space. A parent may plead to be informed

about when teenagers will be home and their whereabouts only to receive evasive, elusive replies.

To the outside observer it can seem that the distancing teen is wanting to get out of the relationship while the pursuing parent desperately wants the relationship to strengthen. It's not always so simple! These relationships are two sides of the same coin. One person's role cannot exist without the other person's. In these complementary see-saw relationships, problems arise when one person takes one end of the see-saw (say, pursuing) while the other always takes the other (distancing). Parents and teens in these relationships become stuck and limited, caught in a repeating loop of despair. It's often accompanied by a trade in impossible deals. Parent and teen make mutually exclusive demands of each other. These impossible deals become the axis of the see-saw and these issues get churned and raked over with terrifying regularity.

I want to be my own person	but	Feed me, fund me and do my laundry
I want you to be home more	and	I also want you to be more independent
I need my own space	but	Clean up after me
My bedroom is sacred private ground	but	I can't find anything to wear
I absolutely trust you	and	Where are you?
I want more freedom	but	You neglect me

Of course, if played out neatly, both parent and teen would become bored and change. Nature has a way of making things interesting, however. As the pressure builds, parents and teens play their usual roles. When tension has reached a critical point, one person storms off (usually the teen) and has a hissy fit. The battle has gone too far. Both retreat to their respective lairs, muttering and cursing and await round two. This pattern is replayed time and time again. With each recurrence, emotional scar tissue builds.

> Being a victim ... can stop teens growing up.

Persecutor–victim see-saws

The other main type of see-saw relationship is where one person becomes the persecutor and the other the victim. Being a victim allows teens to be perpetual adolescents. It stops them growing up. Victims feel resentful and develop a chip on their shoulder. Blaming your parents and not taking responsibility will only get you so far in life.

Teens who see themselves as victims can have problems when they join the workforce. They see bosses as withholding, mean and dismissive. In their future families, victims feel they are neither acknowledged nor loved enough. In romance, they can feel dominated and ruled by a 'replacement' parent. Treating a romantic partner like a parent is destructive and all too common.

Parents can also feel like victims. They are devoting valuable years of their life to a teen who seems ungrateful, uncaring and unpleasant. Being a considerate and loving parent is good; being a self-sacrificing stress martyr is not. Resentment is a trap.

In all these circumstances, victimhood involves a denial of your power to control your life. Victims act as if someone is holding a gun to their head. If there isn't a gun at your head, you can't be a victim. Ask yourself who is holding the gun.

Checklist of signs that you are in a
see-saw pattern

Tick if these occur frequently in your family.

When I am up, they are down
When I am down, they are up ☐

When I want to be close, they want to be distant
When I want some space, they want to be close ☐

When I feel needy, they are strong
When I feel strong, they are needy ☐

When I am upset, they are calm
When I am calm, they are upset ☐

When I am sad, they are angry
When I am angry, they are sad ☐

When I am loving, they are spiteful
When I am spiteful, they are loving ☐

When I am giving, they are taking
When I am taking, they are giving ☐

When I am happy, they are morose
When I am morose, they are happy ☐

If you have acknowledged that one of these see-saw patterns is true of you and your tricky teen, you may now want to leap into changing it. Slow down! For now, it is enough to notice and be aware of it. We'll get to changing it soon.

Escalating relationships

In see-saw relationships, people take opposite roles. In escalating relationships, people do the same thing at once. In these relationships, everyone goes screaming together to the top floor before plummeting to the basement. The same sickening journey is repeated over and over again.

These relationships can have a lot of fireworks. Whether they are sparking in the penthouse or smoldering in the basement, these relationships are still escalators. They are often based on similarity. Like an escalating arms race, both sides head for M.A.D. (mutually assured destruction). It is a pressure-cooker situation. To the outsider, escalating relationships look intolerable and toxic. Behind the intensity, however, lies great connectedness between the parent and the teenager.

> Most people treat relationships like a tennis court.

Most people treat relationships like a tennis court. Their responsibilities only cover their side of the net. If it's on their side of the net, they take responsibility for and fix it. Whatever is on the other side of the net is the other person's doing and not their responsibility. Sounds reasonable, doesn't it? Each person is responsible for their own actions. Yet there is a glitch in this neat and popular way of viewing relationships. There is a human tendency to see our actions as good and blameless and the when problems occur, the other person's actions as self-serving and sneaky. Anything that goes wrong in the relationship is seen as coming from the other side of the net. In escalating relationships, this can really cause fireworks. We apportion blame and despair.

- If only she would be respectful.

- If only he would take responsibility for getting up for school.

- If only she would be honest with me.

- If only he would talk to me about his worries.

We may not always be able to alter other people's actions, but to be powerful in escalating relationships, we need to try. To do this, we need to adopt a view of relationships that may seem unfair and unreasonable. Act as if you are responsible for the entire tennis court. Not just your side of the net but the other side, the fence, the surroundings, the whole box and dice. In others words, assume responsibility for *everything* that happens. This means you will be asking yourself questions like:

- How do I create that aspect of our relationship?

- How do I act differently to create a different outcome?

- What can I do in the future to improve how we get along?

Obviously this has limitations. I'm not suggesting you become a victim and endure violence or abuse. What I am saying is that for most of your relationships with others where direct abuse or violence are not occurring, act is if you are the cause, the creator and at times the solver of anything that happens within that relationship. As delusional as this might sound, it places you in a powerful position to alter and improve your life and the relationships you have with your teen.

Checklist of signs that you are in an escalating pattern

Tick if these occur frequently in your family.

We spark one another off ☐

Whatever the feeling (sadness, anger, hurt, fear), at the end of our interactions they are intensified for us both ☐

At times the intensity of our interactions scares me ☐

I give in sometimes because I feel we have just gone too far ☐

When a third person tries to intervene in our battles it rarely helps ☐

We trade insults that become more and more hurtful ☐

Sometimes we end up screaming at one another ☐

Knowing the see-saw or escalating patterns of relationships places you in a powerful position to improve the relationship. When you have identified the pattern of your relationship, write it in the dossier.

The Tricky Teen Dossier

If you find it difficult to decide, ask people who also know your teen.

My teenager's five main values and priorities are:

1   4

2   5

3

The main communication style they have is as a:
- [ ] Word Trader   [ ] Practical
- [ ] Emotional   [ ] Physical
- [ ] Visual

They mainly receive love through the language of:
- [ ] Quality time   [ ] Physical touch
- [ ] Gifts   [ ] Acts of service
- [ ] Words of affirmation

The filter that they hear most of my communication through is:
- [ ] Controlling   [ ] Critical
- [ ] Unloving   [ ] Selfish

The repeating pattern or our dance around this is:
- [ ] Escalating   [ ] Bit of both
- [ ] See-saw relationship [ ] Unsure

Having now completed the tricky teen dossier, you know more about your teen than most parents and are ready to embark on the six-week process.

Week One – Step back a little!

Before you do anything else, take a break. Unless the situation is immediately and directly life-threatening, the wisest first action is no action. Have a rest.

By stopping whatever you are doing in relation to your teenager's behaviour, you may have already removed half of the problem – your response. Sometimes by continually trying to solve a problem, we unwittingly make it worse. Stepping back is not always straightforward. Sometimes when a parent decides not to intervene, the problem escalates temporarily. This may be because the teen is so used to your response that they will up the ante until they get the response they are looking for.

> Stepping back is not always straightforward.

You've been struggling with these problems for quite a while now. You are possibly feeling exhausted, hurt and disheartened. You also know that if you keep responding in the same old ways you will get the same old results. Sitting back and not intervening for a week allows you to look at the problem with fresh eyes and to consider alternative ways to respond. At some stage during the week, do something pleasant for yourself. The next six weeks will require a lot of you and you need to be ready to tackle it.

Until you have achieved a full week of non-intervention, do not start the six-week process.

A week of non-intervention achieved by sending your teenager to Aunty Vera's or spending a small fortune on them to buy peace doesn't count. To be effective, the week of non-intervention should be during a time when it's life or business as usual.

If you feel the situation is too grave or life-threatening to take a break, get professional assistance for your teenager. If they won't participate, get it for yourself. Life is too short and too precious to spend it panicking. If you get professional help, say something like, 'I don't know if you have a problem or if I have a problem, but I'm worried about you. I need to know if should be worrying or not. I want you to come with me to see someone. You may only need to go once.' It's rare that teenagers refuse to come under those circumstances but if they do, go yourself.

> Now it's time to clear the emotional air.

During this week of resting up and refreshing you may want to consider some of the patterns in your interactions with your teen. Recognising old dance patterns, without blame, puts you ahead of the game. Knowledge is power! You've compiled your teen dossier. Now it's time to clear the emotional air.

Hints for dealing with hurt feelings

After battling with your teen you probably feel hurt. Your help has been unappreciated. Your love has not always been reciprocated. Your requests have fallen on deaf ears. Suffering and feeling hurt are feelings none of us seek out. They are also feelings none of us can avoid. We feel hurt because we care. Robots and machines don't feel hurt. Feeling hurt is understandable, but not useful.

Try to give the issue you are feeling hurt about a value score on a range from 0 to 100 where 100 equals devastating and 0 is not a problem. Then ask yourself:

- Is this issue as important as I think it is?

- Is this as dire and hurtful as I think it is?

- Is my feeling in line with the importance of this issue or have I blown things out of proportion?

Then try to analyse your responses by asking questions like these:

- How can I use these feelings of hurt?

- What can I learn from this?

- If this were a messenger standing at my front door what would the message be?

- Think back to other times you have felt hurt. Do they still feel painful or have they faded with time?

- Now that I have a 'lemon' (difficult time) in my life, how can I make lemonade? How do I make the best of this hurtful situation?

- How can I comfort myself enough so that I can recover?

Recovering from hurt

One way to recover from hurt is to mentally sit beside it as you might beside a close friend in need of comfort. Perhaps you can feel its tenderness and sadness. Perhaps you can relate to its deep sense of disappointment and desolation. Things have not turned out as planned. Love has become a wound. Just sit with hurt. Let it be there. Try not to let it bubble into anger. Anger can alleviate hurt but in the end, it solves nothing. Anger and blame just lead back to more hurt. To sit and gently accept your own deep sense of hurt will strengthen your sense of hurt. If you feel hurt, it is likely that others do too. Your teen's sense of hurt will be expressed away from you but it exists nevertheless. Sitting with hurt eventually takes us towards compassion – for ourselves and for others.

> Don't try to shift or cure your sense of hurt.

Hurt feelings can infiltrate and spoil the best of relationships. Left to fester, hurt can turn into bitterness. It can entrench itself and divide your heart. Don't try to shift or cure your sense of hurt. It is an appropriate feeling after all that has happened. As you sit beside your own hurt, use it to forge your resolve. Use it to create the compassion and the energy needed to build a better relationship. During this week, while you are not intervening, take steps to begin recovering from hurt.

Give up influencing outcomes   No persuasion, no coercion, no consequences, no influence. For this week, let the situation be what the situation is. Let the person be who the person is.

Be slow to judge   After an extended period of battling with a tricky teen, both of you anticipate the other's intentions before anything happens. This type of mind reading is usual in tricky relationships and it is also notoriously inaccurate. Admit your telepathic inadequacies.

Act for the good of others   Use your feeling of hurt to act for the good of others. While you have been embroiled in family dramas, some important people may have been neglected. If there is someone you know who is lonely, visit them. If someone needs a compliment, make it.

Be true to your word   Be the person you intend to be, now. Do what you say you will do. In the heat of disputes with teens your other commitments can fall by the wayside. This is understandable, but is also diminishes your reputation. If there are people who have been let down by you while you dealt with the intensity of your teen's behaviour, now might be a good time to make it up to them.

Avoid criticism   Give it up. Make no negative comments about anyone for this week. Criticism strikes at the hearts of us all but especially teenagers. Criticisms are particularly damaging when they come wrapped in sugar-coated suggestions, hints or considerations for possible improvements.

Be kind   No one likes feeling hurt, but it does help us to relate to how many people feel much of the time. Hurt helps us to feel grounded and humble. Most people you meet are going through a fairly tough time, be kind.

Use the hurt you feel to rebuild the quality relationships in your life.

Week Two – Be clear about what you want

The second week involves sharpening your intentions. It begins with more inaction. Continue not to intervene.

Sharpen your thinking

In a hundred words or less, write out what you think the problem is between you and your teen. I know it is tempting to gloss over these types of tasks. Please don't! They are crucial to identifying the main problem. Write down the problem.

This is the week for thinking about what *you* want. Many parents of tricky teens find themselves being reactive. They respond to the latest drama and try to battle it on all fronts. As a result, they become exhausted and ineffective. Now is the time to write your goal. Write one goal only in three sentences or less. It's often easier to write what you don't want rather than what you do. Change, 'I want him to stop running off from school,' or 'I want her to stop teasing her young brother,' into the positive, such as, 'I want him to attend school,' or 'I want her to be civil towards her brother.'

Live person goals

Goals should be short, precise and be phrased in terms of starting something rather than stopping something. As Russ

Harris so cleverly points out, you need live person goals, not dead person goals. This doesn't just apply to your tricky teen; it applies to you. It applies to New Year resolutions. The key is to never set a goal that a dead person can do faster than you can.

Giving up smoking and drinking? Easy for a dead person.

Losing weight? Not a problem if you're dead.

Being still and not arguing? Easy-peasy if you're dead.

Don't have too many hills to die on

Now that you have determined the goal you are after, it's time to complete the relationship repair kit. But first, look over your goal. Is there any way of making it smaller or more achievable? The larger a goal is the easier it is to miss it. Break it down if possible.

Tricky teens have more energy to put into battles than you do. If you have too many battlefronts they will always win a war of attrition. You will be left exhausted while they are bouncing back for the next round. This is why wise

parents pick their battles very narrowly and very, very carefully. They also use their skills to advantage. Teenagers are all about action and not so much about purpose. Wise parents then act less and become sharply focused on the outcomes they want.

To create a sustainable change in your relationship with your tricky teen, you need to be single minded. Given that the attention of most teens wanders like an inebriated reveller, this will give you a distinct advantage. Decide on your goal and stick with it.

> Teenagers are all about action and not so much about purpose.

Tricky Teen Relationship Repair Kit

- What would I need to improve the relationship?

- What should I stop doing?

- What should I keep doing?

- What should I start doing?

- What would be the first indication to me that the relationship is starting to improve?

Choosing things to do is often easier than deciding what to stop doing. For this reason, find a few ideas on the next page. Circle the things you've already tried that haven't worked. This will remind you not to use them again.

Things parents often do that don't work

Asking for understanding	Yelling	Pleading
Lecturing	Bargaining	Persuading
Supervising homework	Distracting	Avoiding the issue
Saying I'm trying my best	Punishing	Threatening consequences
Stop laundry	Stop cooking	Stop affection
Demanding they spend time with you	Screaming at them to get out of bed	Time out
Spying	Paying them for chores you didn't need done	Sending them to their rooms
Outlining the long-term outcomes	Bribery	Becoming a stress martyr
Demanding they respect you	Not talking to them	Complaining to others about them
Not wanting to upset them	Sleeping less	Worrying more
Getting angry over irrelevant details	Being unnecessarily firmer with other kids	Hiding your feelings

Sarcastic comments	Coercion	Trading insults
Expecting them to read your mind (they should know how I feel)	Thinking that talking to them will upset them	Scaremongering
Making excuses for them	Letting them get out of school	Working even harder to please them

Week Three – Map the dance and go on a treasure hunt!

Over the next few weeks you will be breaking down the old patterns and interactions and laying the groundwork for a new culture of cooperation in your family. While this is happening, you will get fluctuations in behaviour from your tricky teen.

Hold firm. Try to keep in mind that we are not aiming to shift major behavioural patterns over these weeks, we are aiming for something much larger – a new way of relating. By the end of this week things should feel quite different to you and quite weird to your teen. In fact, if your teen suspects that you are in need of psychiatric care by the end of this, well and good.

Mapping how they do their dance

Teenagers do pretty much the same thing in the same way over and over again. As we've discovered, much of their behaviour is led by habits and neurochemistry. Much teenage behaviour boils down to an event or action that triggers a change in neurochemical balance that sets off a series of behaviours that lead to a reward.

Cue → Alterations in neurochemical balance → Routine or dance steps → Reward

It's a familiar progression. The teen is working on something and it gets difficult and they get tired. Their level of dopamine drops so they feel less motivated to get the work finished. They distract themselves with something pleasant, thereby gaining a double-whammy reward – the pleasurable thing and the avoidance of work.

To change this pattern, we could search for the cues or triggers of the dance. The problem is, they may be obscure. The cues may be more to do with your teen's state of being – hard day, sleep deprivation, overdue school assignment, boredom – than anything to do with the present situation.

> Tricky teens do the same dumb thing in the same dumb way over and over again.

If the tricky teen's dance routine is around anger or resentment, the triggers may be internal. These can only be altered if we can predict that they are going into a dance and we can alter their neurochemical balance in time. Having the strategy of feeding or distracting a grumpy kid is a great idea – if you catch the mood early enough.

Searching for the rewards can also lead us on a wild goose chase. It is often not clear if they are after attention, distraction, freedom or expression. Teens are peculiar beings with rewards that are not always evident to the more frontally lobe-endowed members of the population.

So, our best place to begin is the dance routine itself. Tricky teens do the same dumb thing in the same dumb way over and over again. When the pattern or dance routine involves only one person, it is easier to map clearly. When a family is involved, it becomes more complex.

One way to map a parent–teen dance interaction is to draw a map of your home (or wherever the dance occurs) and have different coloured buttons representing all the people involved in the dance. As you do this you may realise that there are other key players in the dance and so you may need to add more buttons for pets, people or objects of value around the house. The process of tracking a dance is to understand it from start to finish. If I was there talking to you about this, I would ask you lots and lots of itsy bitsy questions such as:

- Which room of the house are you in when it begins?

- Is your tricky teen in the room too?

- If not, how do you begin to interact?

- Do they come to you or you to them? In which room?

- Do you move from room to room?

- What is said first?

- What do they do or say?

- What do you do or say?

- Then what happens?

- Then what happens?

- Then what happens?

No detail is too small. Whether you turn left or right, yell or whisper or walk away for a minute may be important. On the map, note where interactions happen and write down roughly what is said. It will take you at least three run-throughs, maybe more, before you get the key dance steps clear in your head. They will vary depending on circumstances, but if you get the key moves down, you can start to alter the steps.

You can map the dance in many ways. You could use textas or crayons and butcher's paper, upturned coffee cups or a white board. If you lay out the dance steps spatially so you view it from above, you will be able to follow the dance more clearly. The sample dance steps that follow may be sickeningly familiar to some families. The brain-numbing repetitiveness of the battle is wearing.

Knowing the dance allows the parents of a tricky teen to remove themselves from the heat of the moment. Even if it is only being able to say, 'Here we go, doing the same old thing again,' it at least gives some perspective. Unlocking the sequence of the dance steps allows us to look for pivotal intervention points but before we do that, we need to lay a little groundwork and look for the dance steps themselves.

> Knowing the dance gives some perspective.

An example dance sequence

We creep in to see this dance occur at 7.30 am.

Scene: A teen is sleeping soundly. The alarm – set for 7 am in order to have the teen attend school and gain an education that will steer him on a pathway to a productive and independent life – has been ignored.

A mother, suspecting her son has spent the night on his computer, paces the kitchen floor, steaming. Mother enters son's bedroom and brightly says, 'You've slept in, Tim. It's time for school.'

Son: Mumbles something incoherent.

Mother leaves room and returns in five minutes with a cup of coffee and says, 'Have a cup of coffee and get up, please.'
Son: (yells) 'Leave me alone.'

Silence throughout the house. No-one stirs. Father bounds up the stairs and remonstrates with son, 'Get up or you'll be late for school. I've got to leave for work so if you want a lift …'

Son: 'Leave me alone! I don't care.'
Father: 'Well, I do care! Get up now or I'll ban the computer for a month.'
Son: (yells) 'You don't understand me.'

Father returns to kitchen (and the argument transfers downstairs).

Mother (to father): 'Do you think he's depressed?'
Father: 'Lazy, you mean.'
Mother: 'You should spend more time with him.'
Father (through gritted teeth): 'Listen, I have a job to go to and he should be at school.'
Mother: 'Yelling at him isn't going to help.'
Father: (angrily) 'I'm leaving for work!'

Whether the dance is about computer time or homework being completed or respect of family rules and standards or the morning rush hour, there will be set steps. The repetition of these patterns grinds parents down. Doing up a shoelace you can handle, but if the shoelace keeps coming undone, we are on a short pathway to fury and frustration. Within this repetition lies the power to create change but before we tackle that, we need to redirect our attention.

Other dances

While the dominant dance of concern or conflict has taken over your family life, other dances have been left unnoticed. These are the times when the problem doesn't happen.

This may be hard to believe, but there are times when your tricky teen is, well, er … nice! There are times when you are also the calm, collected, wonderful person that you glimpse every so often in the photo album. Sadly, these two events rarely coincide when you and your teen are in the same room at the same time.

> There are times when your tricky teen is, well, er … nice!

It's easy for us to gloss over the times of calm or carefree happiness or see them as a brief lull between a series of storms. This is the week to dig deep, to wipe the lenses clean and have a clear new look at things.

Your quest is to find times when the problem doesn't happen.

Don't pay attention or respond when the problem happens – you already know enough about the problem. You have mapped it out in its gory details. The trickier issue is to find out what's going on when the problem isn't around. What's happening when he seems happier? What's going on when she helps around the house or does some schoolwork?

Keep non-problem times firmly in your sights. It's too easy to get sucked back into thinking about the problem and whatever it is that might be causing it. This only blinds you to opportunities for change. If there are things that seem to be happening when the problem isn't there, see if you can make those things happen more often.

Redirect your attention Our energy and effort follow our awareness. Once we focus our attention on something, we tend to create more of it. Go back over the goals you set up and the relationship repair kit and notice any movements made either by your teen or yourself in the directions you set.

Go on a treasure hunt   Despite your more recent impressions, you have possibly raised a remarkable person. They may have concealed their best parts from you. This is the time to go on a search to find talents, skills, contributions, attributes, abilities and interests that your teenager has. Ask them about them. Make much of them. Highlight them. There is gold in teenagers; it is just they have forgotten how to find it.

> *We do not believe in ourselves until someone reveals deep*
> *that inside us something is valuable, worth listening to,*
> *worthy of our trust, sacred to our touch. Once we believe*
> *in ourselves we can risk curiosity, wonder, spontaneous*
> *delight or any experience that reveals the human spirit.*

E.E. Cummings

Week Four – Try out a new dance

The power of yes!

It's going to be hard work getting an argument out of you this week. That is because you are going to be so damn agreeable you'll make Ned Flanders of *The Simpsons* look obstinate. During this week, spend the entire time saying yes to your teenager. Whatever they suggest, agree!

It's simple but scary. They say, 'I want to go to a party.' You say, 'Great idea. I'll get my scarf.' They say, 'I don't want to go to school today.' You respond with, 'OK, what will we do together?' They say, 'I want to go to Mozambique.' You say, 'What a terrific idea. Let's work out a way to do that.' They say, 'I want frog legs and ice cream for dinner.' You say, 'Fantastic – I'll get the ice cream, you find the frogs.'

Get the idea? You'll agree to do almost anything with them. Probably by the end of the week they will be so sick of you being so damn agreeable they'll either think you're on drugs or start seriously thinking about whether you are certifiable.

You have probably spent a considerable portion of the past few months either saying 'No' to your teen or giving hesitant, qualified answers like, 'We'll see.' If this is the case, responding to almost any proposition with an exuberant 'Yes!' should stand out like a beacon. It doesn't mean that you are their slave or dogsbody for a week. You are not going to rush out and buy tickets to Mozambique, but you are going to agree to the idea in principle.

Let me give you an example of agreeing in principle. In 1994 when Kurt Cobain, the lead singer of Nirvana died, a lot of fans were grief stricken. A young teen girl came to see me saying she too wanted to die because she wanted to be like Kurt. I asked her if she played guitar, had a band, wrote songs or toured the world. 'No,' she said, she hadn't done those things. 'So you have a few things to do before you die then, let's work on them,' I said.

Just recently she phoned me to let me know she has launched her CD and is going on tour. 'That's fantastic,' I said and then hesitantly asked, 'Do you still want to die?' 'No,' she said. 'You've got to be kidding.'

Agreeing to ideas in principle sidesteps the battleground and can open up amazing possibilities.

Magical mystery tours

This is a nifty idea that many families can benefit from doing. Tried and tested, it works with many families.

Spring a short, surprise trip on your teen. Invite them to do things with you. Don't tell them about it in advance just say, 'I'd like you to come out with me today there's a few things I've got to do.' If it's a school day, so much the better. Take them out of your local area to lunch or to the movies, the greyhounds, the art gallery, a music event, out to play cards, to test drive new cars that you have no intention of buying – take them to places you wouldn't normally go with them. If they whinge and complain and tell you it's boring, just agree and smile pleasantly.

Do this with each of your children at least once a year. It is an outing they will never forget.

> Spring a short, surprise trip on your teen.

Now, we all know that just ignoring the issues and agreeing with everything they say is not going to create sustainable change, but it does clear the air and give everyone a chance to view things freshly. Taking them on short magical mystery tours is a nice break, but it doesn't shift things long term.

Time travel for parents

When you look at the behaviour of most tricky teens, you could understand it more easily if you subtracted ten years from their current age. A tricky sixteen-year-old can act a lot like a storming six-year-old, a fifteen-year-old can act a lot like a feisty five-year-old and so on. So treat them as if they are ten years younger than their current age – not in a bossy way but in a nurturing way.

It's amazing how teens, especially boys, respond to some of the things we used to do for them when they were younger. Warmed pajamas, bedtime snacks, the smell of fresh towels or sheets, baking a special dish they love or a special wake-up drink in the morning. Perhaps offering to read them a bedtime story might be going a bit too far, but you get my drift.

Create a nurturing environment that will subtly remind them they are loved and cared for. You might also find that you are more powerfully reminded about how much you love and care for them.

Match your teen's preferred love language and communication style

Start practising with the power of language. You've probably been doing this without consciously thinking about it for years. This is the week to really start testing out its power on your tricky teen. To refresh your memory, here they are once more.

Love languages	Communication styles
Quality time	Word traders
Gifts	Emotional
Words of affirmation	Visual
Physical touch	Practical
Acts of service	Physical

And now, here are some ideas about what you can do to match them.

Communi-cation/Love languages	Words	Emotions	Visual	Practical	Physical
Quality time	Long con-versations. Ask more questions	Ask them about their favourite song	Watch a movie	Arrange a holiday, outing or adventure	Be closer, hug if you can
Gifts	Go for coffee and a chat	Write a note about how much you love them	Show them your favourite photos of them	Help them to do something challenging or give a present	Take them to an event they will enjoy
Tell them they are wonderful	Tell them that you love them more	Hug them and express apprecia-tion	Smile when you see them more	An award or certificate thanking them for being them	Pats on the back, thumbs up
Touch	Sit close on a couch and chat or watch a show	Take them to a place that is special for you	Ask them to teach you a computer game	Arrange for them to get a special haircut or make up	Bike rides, bowling, playing games
Help	Tell them how much they mean to you	Tell them what you hope for them in the future	Show them the places that one day you hope they will visit	Sort out a problem or issue for them	Be excep-tionally helpful

These are just some ideas. Tying the activities you do into their interests and values will be even more powerful than these suggestions.

Make most of these interventions short and sweet. In most cases, it's best if the parent puts a time limit on it – 'I've only got half an hour. Would you like to ...' You can even cut the event short, saying something like, 'That was great. I'm sorry I've got to go – let's do it again soon.'

Hit-and-run parenting and saturation bombing

Alongside breezing in and out with activities aligned to their love languages and communication styles, you can also conduct hit-and-run parenting raids with your tricky teen. A moving target is harder to hit and impossible to argue with.

Swoop in with statements like, 'I love you,' 'You're amazing,' 'You're a legend.' Then swoop out. Don't wait for a reply.

> A moving target is harder to hit and impossible to argue with.

This week was designed to break the back of entrenched bad habits. Next week is designed to kick them into history as we dismantle the old dance in earnest.

The treasure hunt you started this week will be built upon next week. Soon you will be as cheerily positive as a giddy aunt after a couple of sherries.

Week Five – Dismantle the old dance

This is the week for rising above the merde. It is the time for implacable parenting. No longer part of their drama, you have taken your sails out of their winds. Now is the time for sustainable consolidation of your relationship with your tricky teen.

You become really unpredictable. If your teenager hasn't already considered you a suitable candidate for serious medication, they will after this week.

Your job is to encourage more of the things that happen when the problem doesn't exist, while doing the reverse of what you did before.

Selecting pivotal points

By now the sequence of tricky teen's behaviour should be familiar:

Alterations in

**Cue → neurochemical → Dance steps → Reward
balance**

The question is where to intervene most effectively? As always, there are many options.

Cues

These are the starter kits. The little devils that start the whole shebang off in the first place. Does it make sense to start here? Nip it in the bud, so to speak? Maybe, maybe not. It's better to put a sign warning people that there is a cliff ahead than to put a trampoline at the bottom of the cliff. Prevention is better than cure.

> We don't always need to know the cause of behaviour.

Your family has been teeming with cues. Angry words, disappointments, despair and worry have been wafting around your house. All the treasure hunting, stopping, looking for alternative dances, analysis of dance steps and noticing positives over the past few weeks have been partially designed to lower the frequency of those cues that create problems in your home.

Don't be misled. They still pack enough of a punch to set off battles that could build into a major war. Lessening the cues that lead to toxic interactions makes good sense, as does increasing those that build a family culture of cooperation (see the section on Arguments on page 49).

We don't always need to know the cues and causes of behaviours in order to understand them. There's an old story about a man who was charged with biting off another man's finger. In court, an eyewitness was being cross-examined. 'Did you actually see my client bite off the finger?' 'No,' the eyewitness replied. 'So how can you be certain that the accused bit the finger off?' the defense lawyer asked. 'Well,' said the eyewitness, 'I saw him spit it out.'

Change the neurochemical balance

Generally high levels of the stress hormones, cortisol and adrenaline, are the culprits and higher levels of serotonin and dopamine are your friends.

Again, to recap:

Avoid	Try to
Demands and time limits	Give choices and options
Sudden changes of plan	Have routines and rituals
Drama and yelling	Be calm and take your time
Critical comments	Express love and praise
Drinking energy drinks and caffeine	Drink water
Too many rules at once	Take it steadily
Late night battles	Get enough sleep
High pressure situations	Have some challenges
Being a couch potato	Do some exercise

Dance steps

The simplest way to alter a tricky teen's behaviour is to alter their routine or dance steps. At times, this will mean changing what they do, at others it will involve changing what you do. Once you have mapped out their dance, you will pretty much know what they are going to do before they have even thought about doing it.

The great news is that to change a dance, you don't have to alter the entire dance. Change one step in the sequence and the whole dance changes. Our habits and routines cluster together. Anger, jealousy, grief and resentment often cluster together. Fear, sleeplessness, avoidance and anxiety often group together. Giving, generosity, consideration and happiness also cluster together.

These clusters hang around pivotal points. To give a slightly bizarre example, I have never seen a heroin-using young person who has not first smoked cigarettes. I am not saying that every young person who smokes cigarettes will go on to use heroin. What I am saying is that if you do a deal with your teenager so they don't smoke cigarettes, it provides strong protection against heroin use.

> It's also important to note that tricky teens change from the outside in.

Risk and protective factors cluster together too. Being out two or more nights a week without your parents' knowing where you are clusters with substance abuse and criminal involvement. Having a diversity of friends protects against being unduly traumatised by bullying which, in turn, clusters with a sense of self-worth and acceptance.

The trick here is working out what are the pivotal points that will topple over a set dance routine thereby improving your family life. It's also important to note that tricky teens change from the outside in. Get them doing something different and they start to think about themselves differently. If that happens, they then start to treat others differently.

Setting out this information is not about lecturing, telling, informing, persuading or enlightening them so that eventually the lights go on, insights occur, they see the error of their misguided ways and act differently. No. By changing what they do and what you do, the dance sequences are altered which opens up opportunities for them to view themselves differently.

By the end of this week, your family interactions should be unrecognisably different from the past. Finding these pivotal points can be a bit of a try-it-out-and-see proposition.

Ways to dismantle the old dance

In choosing how to alter the dance steps, you can either change what your teen does or, if that seems too difficult, you can change what you do. The suggestions outlined below might seem quirky. Some might even see them as manipulative. But 'manipulate' means 'to fix'. You can't leap into a new way of relating unless you jumble up and shake yourself out of an old way of relating. Select changes that are consistent with your values and are strange enough for your teen to consider them to be seriously weird.

Method one: Change the frequency or rate of the problem

Breaking a pattern of speaking faster or s-l-o-w-e-r makes a difference. In heated interactions, people usually speak faster so changing to a slower way of speaking means that teens are more likely to listen to you. The pattern is usually one of people interjecting, interrupting and speaking louder to get their point made, so you need to be prepared to miss your speaking turn for a while. It will be OK. (Although one parent slowed down her rate of speaking so much her teenage daughter became worried she was having a stroke.)

It is also worth considering increasing the amount of time you give teenagers to reply to you. When family life gets rushed and we get ignored, there's a tendency to launch into a tirade after a moment's silence. Teens, especially boys, often require more time than adults to process information. It takes time for the penny to drop. Standing, looking quizzically at them, while silently counting to one hundred can be a good way to begin. When we slow down, we become aware of subtle signs that we may have missed.

Method two: Change the timing

If you feel you have become too consistent and predictable, you could just decide to respond in two different ways on alternate days. Life with a tricky teen can be hectic, dramatic and chaotic. Rituals and routines vanish into thin air. Review the issue sheet on the ideal day and consider what time things should occur in your family.

An extreme example of this was a family who was tired of the squabbling and conflict that occurred at the rush hour of every school morning. The parents decided to have the main meal for the day at 6 am. If you weren't there, you missed out. It took a few torrid weeks with some fairly hungry kids before they altered their timing.

You can also delay the response time to alter a habit. One of the most effective ways to help people to lose weight is to ask them to write down everything they eat before they eat it. Another is a slight delay in eating. If you crave chocolate, write down your degree of desire on a scale of 0–10 and the set an alarm for 15 minutes. When the alarm goes off, make a conscious decision by asking yourself if you still want chocolate. Giving some tricky teens a choice of chores and a time within which to make a decision about which one to do is another effective strategy.

Method three: Change the duration of problem

This is really good for complaints and teens who say, 'You don't understand me.' The next time they say, 'You don't listen,' or 'You don't understand me,' say, 'Right! You've got ten minutes. Tell me.' Sit them down and for ten minutes, utter not one word. Listen intently to whatever they want to say, for ten minutes. Do not interrupt. Make no comments. At the end of ten minutes, say, 'Thank you dear – I now understand.' Get up and walk off. After this they shouldn't be able to say they haven't been heard but if they do, repeat the intervention.

Method four: Change the location of the problem

As most teen behaviour is habitual, any shift has the potential to jolt the dance out of its usual pattern. One of the most powerful changes is to alter its location. Insisting that if your teen wants to argue they should do it only in front of the television can be interesting. One family, worn out by trying to cajole their teenage son out of bed in the morning, decided to breakfast in his bedroom for a few weeks accompanied by a radio and animated discussion. (Be careful about your selection of location, however – one family who insisted arguments happen on the front porch saw the police arrive.)

Method five: Add a new element

Habits run on automatic so as soon as you add a new element to the dance, it changes. I'll never forget the angry teenage boy who hit trees. It was apparent that he was also a nationalistic character and so I asked him for a week to avoid hitting native trees and to instead take his anger out on the introduced species. He came back saying, that he was, 'sick of looking for trees.'

A daughter complained to her father that he forgot to pack her lunch for school. This was despite her being a strapping and capable young woman. The next day the father rented a tuxedo, prepared lunch and waited in the schoolyard carrying a tablecloth, napkins, a picnic basket and a deferential attitude for his daughter to arrive. For some reason the daughter never complained about lunch ever again.

Method six: Change the sequence of events

This is particularly useful if you think you may have slipped into that parenting technique that is called, in coarser quarters, nagging. This might seem like a slight shift but it can be quite powerful. Reminding your teens to remind you that you need to ask them something sounds obscure. Here's how it might work.

Parent: 'I know I had to ask you about something … now what was it?'

Teen (glumly): 'Doing homework, I suppose.'

Parent (sounding puzzled): 'No that wasn't it but tell me about the homework too, will you?'

Don't use this too often or they will start planning your entry into a home for the demented. Nevertheless it can raise an issue without a full-on battle.

Method seven: Break the pattern into small elements

The attention span of some tricky teens is very short. For this reason it can be useful to practise drip-feed parenting. This is where you seed a small idea, move away, come back, build on it slightly, move away, come back, and build it further. For example, if there is a school assignment coming up and your teen is averse to completing such tasks or waits till the very last evening to cram. Rather than building up a head of stream as the days flit past, mention the smallest segment that they should be working on.

Another way of breaking the pattern into small elements is to take five. In heated moments, having a five-minute time-out signal that can be used to lower the temperature of disputes can also be useful.

Method eight: Change the arena of battle

This is useful for entrenched, stuck battles. Shift the area of concern. A mother whose seventeen-year-old daughter wasn't working at school or attending often, gave up trying to convince her daughter of the usefulness of getting an education. Instead, she started talking to her about how to find a rich husband to support her and mentioned several (fictional) men at her work who might be interested. The mother even left information about dating sites lying around. The daughter confided in me with a shudder that her mother was trying to set her up with 'some old, rich creep'. Interestingly, the daughter started to work at school and did well.

Method nine: Change the response to the problem

This may seem a bit sneaky, but it involves consciously misinterpreting the intention of an action and responding differently. One parent who found that remonstrating with arguing kids wasn't working changed her ways. She would go to the perceived instigator with a worried look on her face and say, 'You must be so sad and unhappy to be fighting with your sister. Let me give you a hug.' A father's experience provides a nice example of this approach.

'I spent hours telling my son how important homework was, I lectured and lectured. The more I told him, the less he did. So I stopped telling him and waited. I noticed that he got panicked when a big assignment was due but left everything to the last minute. So one Sunday night when he told me he had a major assignment due the next day, I said fantastic and dragged him out to a movie instead. I really enjoyed the movie except for the bits when he pleaded with me that this assignment was really important. I said, 'OK, I'll help you when we get home. It took us all night to get the assignment finished. I buttoned my lip the whole time and just encouraged and helped out.

The next day after school when I asked him how we'd gone, he actually thanked me and suggested that next time we should go on a Saturday rather than a Sunday night.'

> Another way of breaking the pattern into small elements is to take five.

Method ten: Change the meaning of the problem

This method is probably most useful when the entire family agree there is a problem. One family had a problem with their teenage daughter, who was so anxious about her parents, she would check on them in the middle of the night, often waking them. We worked with the daughter to reduce and treat her anxiety, but it was clear the parents needed their sleep. We decided that if the parents woke when the daughter crept into her parents' bedroom, they would pretend they'd seen a ghost. After several nights of this, the family burst into laughter as they mocked a horror scene.

Week Six – Build a sustainable relationship

Congratulations! You've made it through six long weeks of shifting the dance you have had with your teens. Hopefully, you've found it rewarding but you have also probably found it exhausting. If you've been coping with a tricky teen, you may find yourself feeling a little (or a lot) depressed. Depression often involves shutting down aspects of your life, turning your focus inwards, being less aware of the present and wary of close intimacy.

The resilient parent

The lesson that tricky teens can teach you is to grow as a person. In a family, everyone grows up, even the parents. Even if you don't feel like you have put your life on hold, it is time for you to grow.

Rediscover who you are

Dealing with teens is wearing and all-consuming. Look for people or areas in your life that you have neglected while your intense interactions with the tricky teen have dominated. It's time to regain the territory. You may have become a hazard to other people. If you have been using people in your life as sounding boards or the complaints desk about your tricky teen, stop.

Recapture your spirit

Invite the valued people in your life to do fun things with you. Recognise that you may have been coming across as full of complaints yourself so understand if people are reticent to begin with. Regardless of whether they initially accept or decline, keep making invitations. Increase intimacy with people you care about. Love people as much as you can.

> Mothers are especially prone to label themselves as failures.

Nourish and increase your strengths

Parents of tricky teens often feel guilty, despondent and worthless. Mothers are especially prone to label themselves as failures. Single mothers even more so. Feeling guilty isn't going to help you and it certainly isn't going to help your teen. It is also not an accurate portrayal of who you are. Take a good, long, hard look at yourself.

- What parts of yourself are your strengths?

- What do people like about you?

- What makes you a good friend?

- What do you value about you?

- What parts of you have gone 'missing in action'?

Make a commitment and an action plan to display those characteristics to the world. Start with people that you feel confident with. There is nobility in living by your highest ideals. Nobility and caring can provide an antidote to the shabby behaviour shown by some tricky teens.

Amplify and market

This involves being more you. Amplify those aspects of yourself that you value. Act as if you are conducting a public relations campaign on yourself. Give yourself time to do this. During this time, try to be close to people.

Change yourself first

One of my favourite Chinese proverbs is, 'People who wait for roast duck to fly in mouth will wait long time.' Tricky teens can put you in a position where you are standing with a gaping mouth waiting for the roast duck. It's not coming. Once you realise this, you will see it everywhere. You'll catch people waiting passively for others to change the situation. You'll find yourself waiting for that passing duck. Think to yourself, 'No roast duck coming in,' and get on with your life.

> Often the person most likely to change is you.

The behaviour of tricky teens may be unfair, unjust, unwarranted and out of order, but that doesn't mean that they'll change of their own accord. Often the person most likely to change is you. The behaviour of tricky teens may not be likeable, but it is important to recognise that they have only a limited repertoire of ways of relating to others. In a fair world, the tricky teen would gain insight into their mean and nasty ways and either get their comeuppance or come to you apologising and begging for forgiveness. Would you like to place a bet on the likelihood of this happening?

The world is not fair. People don't get what they deserve; they get what they look for. You have probably met people who look for betrayal in others and end up with jealousy, some look for defiance and end up trying to control. Yet others look with suspicion and end up with wariness and cautiousness. Look for the best in your teen and they will try to live up to it.

Dealing with a tricky teen can drag us down to their level. You can start acting like a tricky teen yourself. The dramatics, histrionics, the grumpiness and the petulance are not really you. You may start seeing the worst motives in other people. Detoxifying yourself from the effect of tricky teens means regaining a real-world view of others that allows you to see good intentions in trustworthy people.

Expect to feel discomfort

If you have been oppressed or bullied by tricky teens for some time, your new act may feel weird and uncomfortable. Changing yourself takes a bit of getting used to, for you and those

> Don't expect them to give up their ground easily.

around you. Expect to be beset by anxious feelings and thoughts of inauthenticity as a parent – 'I'm not as strong as I'm pretending to be.' The new you may take some time to have an effect on the tricky teen's behaviour. You have training wheels on in this new role. That is why we've spelt out a six-week process for changing. Persist and remain true to yourself.

Expect a response from the tricky teen

Tricky teens adopt behaviours because they work for them. Their behaviour meets their short-term objectives. Acting in these ways gives them a sense of power and alleviates their anxieties. Over time, their ways become a success, their usual way of dancing with their family. They've spent years crafting their ways. Don't expect them to give up their ground easily.

In fact, for a time they may get worse! They may get angrier, sneakier or more controlling. They may try to make you feel mean-spirited for refusing to play their games their way. Some tricky teens may be so unused to parents not giving into them they may burst into tears, throw tantrums or threaten to run away. The teen is used to a diet of partial and intermittent reinforcement. This is a powerful addiction where your behaviours are rewarded every so often. When you get a whiff of success at irregular intervals, you get hooked on the behaviours that led to it. Tricky teens think that if they persist you will give in. Up till now it is likely the evidence is on their side.

> Having the courage to stand up to and deal with a tricky teen is worth celebrating.

Stand still and stand firm. The only people who really like changes are babies. Keep your resolve. Get support from others to help you through this stage.

Celebrate

Some parents survive tricky teens by distancing themselves. They might immerse themselves in work, telling themselves the teen doesn't really want them around anyway or that they need to stand on their own two feet. This strategy is successful but leaves the parent feeling the loss of a cherished and close relationship with their child. Behind the words of bravado lurks great sadness.

Having the courage to stand up to and deal with a tricky teen is worth celebrating. Find a good friend and have a celebratory drink with them and share your story (briefly).

Value relationships over power

One of the great lessons tricky teens can teach us is that coping with anxieties and insecurities by exerting power over others doesn't work. It might buy a short-term advantage but extracting leverage over others never works out well long-term. A great example is one of history's trickiest parents – Joseph Stalin. After his son attempted suicide but survived, his comment about his son Yakov was, 'He can't even shoot straight.'

Practise having a kind heart

Tricky teens can infect you with a feeling of wariness, distrust and suspicion about the motives of others. Take time to look for the best in others and to view them compassionately.

Altering the dance creates an opening for new ways of behaving. Hopefully the past few weeks has given you a chance to create new ways of understanding and relating to your tricky teen.

If after six weeks you are still stuck, it may be time to get some professional assistance. This may be needed if there is a risk to the long-term welfare of the family, in situations of physical violence, depression, self-harm or suicidal acts. People do get better with help.

Essential conversations to have with your teens

The conversations

If we don't transform pain, we transmit it. It echoes and reverberates for some families down the generations.

All teenagers suffer some pain during this stage of life. Partly this is caused by the loss of innocence of childhood. Things are never quite the same as a teenager as they were when you were a child. Tricky teens convert their pain and anxieties into shifty manoeuvres that appear to alleviate the problem in the short-term, but only lead to substantial problems later on.

Teens need our love most when they deserve it least. It is often when they are acting in the most obnoxious ways that they need their parents to be powerfully positive. It takes a highly resilient parent to rebuff the toxicity that some of these teens dish out. To withstand the taunts, challenges and emotional rejection transmitted by these teens and to come back smiling and positive is truly angelic work.

In the course of raising a tricky teen, relationships often become frayed and essential conversations are overlooked as a battle of wills dominates. Hopefully, the process of changing the dance steps of your tricky teen's behaviours has also helped you to become more proactive and intentional. But in the hurly-burly world of raising teens, many essential conversations don't occur because there's too much heat in the relationship or there's too much pressure on all concerned.

Now that you've created a more peaceful family life, this chapter aims to help you find opportunities to create the most essential conversations with your teen. It's time to bring heart, love and values back to the centre of your relationship with your teenager. It's time to fulfill the pledge at the beginning of this book, 'As a parent I am responsible for raising you to be a decent, successful human being who treats themselves and others with tolerance and respect.'

The key conversations all parents should have with their teens is a matter of opinion. Different emphases occur across cultures, at different times and in different countries. You may disagree with some of the conversations I suggest. If you disagree with an aspect of this chapter, consider what conversation you would replace it with. The following conversations have the capacity to transform pain into positive power. Sometimes you will get the rare opportunity to sit down with your teen and discuss one of these issues.

> Transform pain into positive power.

When one of these times crops up, grab it. It's an opportunity to give your teen the words that will enable them to see new worlds. You can't enter a world if you don't have the words to imagine it. It's hard to develop harmonious positive relationships unless you have an idea that such a thing is possible. The example of your own life and how you live it is also a powerful way of having these conversations without words.

Essential conversation 1 – The golden rule

The idea that people who treat others well tend to be treated well in return is one that may have escaped the attention of angry teens. There is a reciprocity about human relationships.

You tend to get back what you give and then some. This is the basis of many caring human friendships.

One of the very few premises all the world's religions and most of the philosophers agree upon is to treat other people as you would like to be treated yourself. This is known as 'the golden rule' and is the basis of civilised society. You could express it as 'Pat my back and I'll pat yours,' or as The Beatles so beautifully put it, 'The love you take is equal to the love you make.'

A cynical tricky teen may well ask, 'Is the golden rule true?' They may have experienced times when they were caring and positive, only to be hurt or rejected in return, particularly at school. Most of us have experienced something similar. So the honest answer is no, the golden rule is not always true. Treating other people well does not guarantee that you will always be treated well. It is difficult to predict other people's actions. But the alternative to the golden rule is a dog-eat-dog mentality. Might is right. The toughest, meanest person wins the prize. This leads to unsatisfying relationships based on fear.

> Most people measure their happiness by the quality of their relationships.

If you regard the person with the biggest bank account, the most shoes, the most intimidating manner or the corner office to have the best life, then maybe the dog-eat-dog approach has some merit. Just don't expect a lot of sympathy when they come for you with bigger weapons than yours.

Most people measure their happiness by the quality of their relationships. The most powerful way to build good relationships is to treat people well. For this reason, it makes sense to begin with the golden rule.

Essential conversation 2 – Forgiveness

Teen: So if I start acting in accordance with the golden rule and other people treat me badly, what do I do then?

You: Forgive them.

Teen: Forgive them! Shouldn't I get back at them, show them how hurt I am, prove to them how nasty and mean they've been? Won't they take me as a soft touch and use me?

You: Forgiveness is the most powerful way of moving beyond past hurts. None of us can change the past, but we can all influence our future. By forgiving past hurts committed by others, you free yourself to move on and create your own future. Forgiveness is a gift to yourself. Otherwise you carry bitterness and resentment around with you.

Buddha compared holding onto anger to grasping hot coals with the intent of throwing them at someone else. Guess who gets hurt while you are holding them?

Teen: But what if I forgive someone and they continue to be nasty?

You: When to collaborate and when to compete is an interesting decision for us all. People are much more attuned to pick up cheating than acts of kindness. We are probably too vigilant about being taken advantage of. Our brain even processes the sense of pleasure and the sense of wariness about being cheated in different areas.

One idea that people commonly use as a guide is 'tit for tat'. This idea is that I will behave towards you as you behave towards me. In tit for tat, you start cooperating, and if the other person cooperates, you continue to cooperate. If the other person cheats, you cheat in return. The next time, if the other person cooperates, you go back to cooperating.

Tit for tat works because:

- It feels nice.

- It starts with cooperation.

- It retaliates if you do something mean to it.

- It is forgiving.

- It is clear in the rules.

In the overall scheme of things, tit for tat is a fairly good way of deciding when to compete and when to collaborate. To give a minor example, you say 'good morning' to someone every day. If they reply and greet you, you greet them the next day. If one day they ignore you, you ignore them the next day.

> Decide when to compete and when to collaborate.

There are limitations to tit for tat, however. The first is that it means that your actions and behaviours are largely dictated by what someone else does. If they ignore you, you end up imitating them. The second problem occurs if a wrong signal is sent or misinterpreted. If a helpful gesture is interpreted as rude, you can prematurely end a collaborative or positive relationship. If you cheerily greet someone and say 'good morning' and they ignore you, you could decide, 'That's it. I will ignore them from now on,' and feel snubbed.

But here is where forgiveness comes in. There may be reasons the person ignored your greeting. They could be unwell, have hearing problems, be distracted or very upset. In this case, the best strategy is 'forgiving tit for tat', where you set up a collaborative relationship. If the other person appears to cheat or not respond or be overly competitive, your initial response is to continue being collaborative.

Teen: But what if they continue to ignore me or be mean to me?

You: Before you decide to treat them as shabbily as they appear to be treating you, think about the sort of person you want to be. Obviously, you don't want to be someone everyone can just walk over and take advantage of. You can think about how you want to treat people in your life and live up to that standard, though. As lots of people live by tat for tat rather than forgiving tit for tat, by acting in accordance with your standards and values, you will help lots of people to have positive relationships.

Forgiveness doesn't mean that you don't look after your own interests. It means that you look for the best in other people and especially in yourself.

Teen: OK, so how do I go about forgiving people? They are going to think I am pretty weird if I start going up to them and say, 'I forgive you.'

You: There are a number of ways we can forgive. Not all them involve talking about it. In a way, forgiveness is a gift that we give ourselves to free us from the hurt of others' wrongdoings. You could:

- Write a forgiveness note to someone in a diary or journal.

- Be grateful for what they can teach you. Sometimes our fiercest competitors are our best teachers. They can teach us to bring out the best in ourselves.

- Forgive yourself. Often we are toughest on ourselves. Acknowledging that you did the best that you could is important. Of course, that doesn't mean you can't learn from this event or improve in future.

- Write it out, sing it out, paint or draw it out, dance it out. Lots of wrong-doings can be turned into creative acts.

- Make a practice of forgiveness. Each day complete a review and see if there is anyone who you felt treated you meanly or badly. Forgive them for it. Then make an intention to treat them well the next time that you see them. Put forgiving tit for tat into practice.

Forgiveness doesn't mean excusing unacceptable behaviour. Rather, it is something you do for yourself. Forgiving people are happier and are less likely to be depressed, anxious, neurotic and angry. They are also healthier. Practising forgiving tit for tat results in lower stress responses – a lower heart rate, lower blood pressure and a less furrowed brow.

Essential conversation 3 – Sincerity, or why apologies matter

Most tricky teens have gone through the motions, making an insincere apology. The word 'sorry' may have left their lips, but it was accompanied by rolling eyes, a contorted face and the tone of the word was dripping with sarcasm or insincerity.

False apologies are like a slap in the face. As their parent you may put up with it, but delivering a poor apology is enough to get you sacked, enough to lose a friendship or the love of your life.

At times it's reasonable for a parent to withdraw privileges until their teen apologises convincingly for an inappropriate remark or action. Learning the power of a sincere apology for a tricky teen is a useful life lesson. Being able to say sorry and mean it, is part of taking responsibility for our actions. Apologising involves understanding that some wrong or hurt has been created by us.

Teen: Why should I apologise?

You: Everyone has moments when they do or say things that hurt other people. Sometimes we do this without even intending to. If the issue is left without an apology, that hurt often grows (unless the person is practicing forgiveness – see last conversation) and the relationship becomes tense or falls apart. We have a responsibility to repair relationships when we have done something to damage them.

Teen: But there were wrongs on both sides, why should I apologise?

You: I would like you to activate the hero that is within you. Be the bigger person and take responsibility for apologising and making amends.

Teen: How do I make a sincere apology?

You: Generally, people want to see you acknowledge your mistakes. Make a brief statement that includes the pronoun 'I' and does not include the word 'but'. For example:

- I'm sorry I said those things about your friend.

- I didn't mean to upset you. I can see that I did, and I want you to know I am really sorry that happened.

- I'm sorry we had that disagreement. I shouldn't have got angry and I want to apologise to you.

Short and to the point is best. Don't try to explain your actions or words. If the person wants an explanation, they can ask you. Don't try to say that your actions were understandable given the circumstances. Don't make excuses. Don't try to make a joke about it so that the other person can laugh their way out of it. It won't work.

At this point, you can end the conversation and plan to check in with the person fairly soon. If you're feeling confident, you might like to suggest that you are prepared to make the issue as good as it can be – 'I'd really like to fix this between us, I'm not exactly sure what I can do, do you have any suggestions?'

> Once an apology is made, don't expect anything in return.

At this point, the other person may have plenty of suggestions of how you could improve your behaviour in the future. Having asked for it, you need to listen to this without defending or excusing yourself. Listen to all of their ideas and then say, 'Thank you. That gives me some ideas to work on.' At this point, you can either finish the conversation or say, 'I hope you'll forgive me.'

Once an apology is made, don't expect anything in return. The other person is not obliged to be understanding or to receive you warmly.

Also, stay with the issue that's the problem. Don't over-apologise. Apologising for everything that has ever happened between you and another person, or for all your previous rudeness, has a lot less impact than focusing on the situation you're taking responsibility for. Also, don't embark on a discussion of your limitations as a human being. Saying something like, 'I'm sorry, I'm such a thoughtless, rude, inconsiderate person,' keeps the focus on you and can ruin a sincere apology.

Essential conversation 4 – Success and a good life

Many teens seem to believe that to be successful, they need to be fabulously rich and popular. Being a celebrity is equated with a happy, successful life. This is despite overwhelming evidence to the contrary.

Teen: I want to be rich and famous.
You: Well, that sounds good. Do you mean rich or wealthy?
Teen: Huh, what's the difference?
You: Being rich is often thought about in terms of dollars. While the amount of dollars you have can relate to having a happy and successful life, it doesn't always work out that way. In fact, once you've got enough money to survive reasonably, getting more money doesn't make you happier.

Wealth is the accumulation of possibilities. A wealthy person has the ability to pretty much choose the life that they want. They may have dollars in the bank, but they also have good friendships, close relationships and the ability to follow their passions in life.

Teen: Well, I want to be both rich and wealthy then!
You: OK, but you might want to think about which one you are going to put your energies into. I've met people who are rich but are not wealthy. These are people who work hard and are often so busy they don't have the time to enjoy the benefits of their money. They work so hard that they rarely get time to see friends or family. On holidays, they are so wound up they can't relax. There's not a lot of point being rich if you're not enjoying yourself. I've also met people who are not financially well off, but are really happy. I guess, in a way, they

are wealthy. Also, if you are happy doing whatever you are doing, you are more likely to become both wealthy and rich.

Teen: How come?

You: If you set out to do something that makes you happy, you tend to do it well. As you enjoy what you do, you find it easier to do more of it. The more you do something, the more skilled you become. Because many people aim to become rich rather than wealthy, they don't specialise in an area they enjoy. If you aim to be wealthy instead, fairly soon you will end up being one of the most skilled and sought-after people in the world in that area.

Teen: So if I want to be wealthy, I should follow my passions?

You: Sure. It takes hard work, persistence and luck as well. But the best way to set yourself up to be truly wealthy is to find something that you are passionate about and do it. It's about finding and following your own path – not about fulfilling someone else's dreams.

Teen: What about fame?

You: There is an old Chinese saying that seeking fame is like a pig seeking slaughter. Magazines like to depict famous celebrities as having wonderful lives and they also show them when relationships break up, diets go bust and troubles hit them hard. Being famous has an upside, but it also has a big downside.

Teen: I don't believe you. Fame has to be good!

You: Think about what it would be like to be celebrity for a moment. Sure, you get invited to exclusive events, but every time you walk down the street someone has a camera on you. If you're sloppily dressed, it will end up the magazines. If you've lost weight, you'll be labelled anorexic. If you've gained weight, you'll be called fat. If you're with someone, you've either hooked up or you're cheating. You no longer have any privacy. Part of the reason famous people buy big mansions or properties is to get away from the prying eyes of the paparazzi. Being wealthy doesn't require fame. In fact, it gets in the way.

Teen: OK, so how do I find out what I am passionate about?

You: It can take a while. Some lucky people discover their passions early in life. The school years aren't the easiest time to discover your passions. Deadlines, tests and social pressures all get in the way. The trick is to live life as broadly as you can and to keep a watch out for things that really captivate you.

Essential conversation 5 – Gracious living, or losing and winning well

Teen: I want to be the best.

You: Then you will have to learn how to lose and how to make mistakes. Everyone wants to win, but no-one wins all the time. The best sports teams don't win every game. The best musicians have off nights. The best people have moments when they are not at their best. The best painters don't produce masterpieces every time they paint.

No one starts out as a master in their field. Everyone has to learn by training, making mistakes, correcting them and improving. For this reason, it's how people lose and respond to losing that will determine how good they will become.

Teen: Huh? I said I wanted to be the best, not the worst – not a loser!

You: If winning were truly the only thing, then there would be no problem with hurting other people, cheating, lying or stealing to win. The world has a very poor opinion of people who cheat in order to win. If you really want to enjoy what you do, shift the focus from winning to giving your best and to having fun.

Teen: Why do I have to lose?

You: When we start to learn anything for the first time, we make mistakes many more times than we get it all perfectly right. We learn more by losing than we do from winning, if we have the courage to pay attention.

Teen: Well, if I lose every so often, can't I just blame bad luck, poor umpiring, the weather or the other person?

You: You could, but you'll miss a great opportunity to be the best if you do that. Blame gets in the way of improvement. It doesn't really matter if you blame the other person, the weather, the umpire or yourself – blame removes your focus from what you can learn in order to do better next time.

If you don't get the mark you want on a test, you could blame yourself and think that you are not smart enough or you could think about how you could prepare differently to get a better result next time. If you focus on improving rather than the result, you are less likely to be depressed and give up when times are tough.

> We learn more by losing than we do by winning.

Teen: And what happens when I win?

You: Enjoy it and also analyse it. Go through your performance and highlight the bits you were pleased with and also the areas you could improve on. Every performance will have a bit of both. Make a plan to practise on improving the parts you feel you could have done better on.

Teen: OK, so how do I lose well?

You: It is important not to throw a fit when you lose. It's also important not to boast when you win. The first thing to do after losing is to congratulate the winner. Always say, 'Congratulations' to the winner. It says a lot about the character of a person that they can accept defeat well and honour the winner. When you win, always mention something about how the other person performed and thank them for playing against you. It is often the people we compete with, regardless of whether we win or lose, that help us to become better.

> It isn't easy to shift a self-centred, tricky teen towards being empathic and compassionate.

Essential conversation 6 – Empathy and compassion

It isn't easy to shift a self-centred, tricky teen towards being empathic and compassionate. We live in a world that rewards celebrity, appearance and money. The earlier you start building empathy, the better. Involving children and teens in helping others around the house, caring for animals, babysitting and volunteering are good places to begin.

As I write this, I can feel some of you rolling your eyes and thinking, I have as much chance of getting my teen to lift a finger to help anyone as I do of holidaying on Mars. Don't despair. Teens want to help people even if they don't realise it. Start off by making small requests of them and be undeterred by their negative responses. Be careful, though. There is a fine line between making requests for help and being bossy. A request may either be accepted or denied.

Assume a willingness to help that may not be matched by any evidence for a while. Slowly aim to increase the sense of helpfulness in the home and eventually broaden this to your community. If you get a chance to have a conversation along the following lines, grab it.

Teen: Why should I care about other people?

You: Well, if you like having friends, it's a good idea to practise empathy. Empathy is the ability to understand the feelings of other people. I guess we all look to our friends to help us understand the times in our lives when things are tough, as well as the times when things are good. Having empathy can be painful for us but then again, so are loneliness and isolation.

> Teens want to help people even if they don't realise it.

Teen: If empathy is painful, what's in it for me?

You: Plenty! People who are empathic seem to have more friends and enjoy their friendships more. Generally, they live happier more satisfying lives.

Teen: So all I need to do is say to someone, 'You seem stressed' or 'What a downer' and that makes me a good friend?

You: Well, there's more to good friendship than just sharing someone else's pain, but it's a start. It also helps to be kind, to be fun to be with and to be compassionate.

Teen: So how is compassion different from empathy?

You: It's good to feel someone else's pain and acknowledge it. This ability to put yourself in someone else's shoes, to see life from their point of view is empathy. Being compassionate is being prepared to do something to help another person feel less pain.

Just being empathic means you share the pain and bad times, but being compassionate means you also get to feel good about yourself for helping someone out. Compassion generally involves reaching out to someone else.

Teen: But lots of people say, 'Look after No. 1.'

You: Looking after yourself is fine but if that's all we did, we'd live in a heartless, lonely and uncaring world. The world seems a better, happier place when people are caring and connected.

Teen: Sometimes you've said that I've been selfish. How do you know I am able to be empathic and compassionate?

You: There is a hero within you that at times, I think you forget is there. Even though you hide it by pretending to be uncaring and tough, I know you care deeply about people. There have been times when you've looked out for other people's interests even more than your own and there are times you have helped out when you didn't have to. The decision you have to make in your life is how much of that hero within you you are prepared to show the world.

Teen: But the world can be a tough, mean place. Can you be too empathic and compassionate?

You: It's good to be sensitive and tuned into other people's emotions and worries. The world needs more sensitive and emotionally intelligent people. Some people can get burdened by their own sensitivity. They become upset at the thought of anyone experiencing hardships. It can paralyse them. They feel upset but can't do anything to help others. Others eventually become so overwhelmed they have to harden themselves up. Some people call this compassion fatigue. Some of these people become cynical and can feel that everyone is out to use them in some way.

Being empathic and compassionate doesn't mean sacrificing yourself. In fact it's important to look after yourself so you can be at your best when you need to be.

Essential conversation 7 – Why it is important to be honest

Tricky teens have often become accustomed to being slippery with the truth. Some begin to believe that the truth is anything they can make other people believe regardless of accuracy or veracity. Admittedly, we all tell white lies. Telling someone who looks like they need a compliment that they are looking great when they really look like they could do with six weeks on a health retreat could be a kindness, but it can also be denying them some important feedback.

Teen: Why should I tell the truth? Why does it matter?

You: Whether to be honest or not is a basic decision you need to make. One reason you might decide to be honest is that people look to their relationships for people they can rely on and trust. People are often wary of anyone they feel might be taking advantage of or lying to them. Being happy usually involves having positive, uncomplicated relationships with those who you love and are important to you. Not being honest can destroy those relationships at worst, but even at best, it threatens the closeness and intimacy you have with those people.

Another reason is that people are not as good at lying as they think they are. Women are generally better at deceit than men, but both give themselves away. If you're going to lie, do it over the phone. Otherwise your body signals will show that you are fibbing.

Teen: But you've lied for me. Do you remember that time you told school I was sick when you wanted us to go away for a long weekend?

You: Yes, I did and it was wrong of me to do so. That time I gave you a bad example. In fact, I'm not sure the teacher really believed me and I felt our relationship had a question mark over it after that. If I had my time again I wouldn't have done it.

Teen: So I should go around telling the truth? Saying, 'You're fat', 'You need to stop drinking', 'Stop sleazing on your best friend's partner'? I'd be an outcast in a day!

You: Being honest doesn't give you a licence to become an insensitive yobbo. You can certainly withhold negative judgements and comments. The most important things to be honest about are not your thoughts about others but about yourself. Having people know where you stand on important issues and how you positively feel about them are the most essential things to be honest about.

Essential conversation 8 – Integrity and reputation

Tricky teens, especially those who have been at war with their parents, often feel that the world should just accept them as they are. Some consider manners, courtesies and making a good impression as a false social artifice.

Teen: Why should I care about what other people think of me? I am who I am!

You: One of the most precious parts of your life is your reputation as a person. It dictates who will be friends with you, who will ignore you and who will help you. A good reputation is a treasure that can be built up over a lifetime or can be ruined in an instant. Guard it carefully. Of course you need to remain true to yourself, but that doesn't mean you can't bring the best of yourself to the forefront of people's attention.

Teen: But aren't there people who are just going to hate me or dislike me?

You: Yes. There are people that are going to hate you, envy you and dislike you for no real reason. They will make up a reason for their feelings. It may be the way you smile, your haircut or just because you seem happy or successful. These people won't change their opinion by anything much you can do. Try not to let them preoccupy you. Focus instead on the open-minded people who you want to have productive, positive relationships with.

Teenage girls sometime believe everyone should like them all the time and that it is a total disaster if someone doesn't like them.

Teen: So how do I protect my reputation?

You: The best way is to be known as a likeable person that others can rely on. Build up your street cred as a good person. As you go through life, some people will want to tear you down. Just as you will gain friends, you will also gain some enemies. If your reputation takes a hit, don't ignore it. No-one is completely safe from reputation attacks and all of us make mistakes from time to time. People who are your enemies will attack you behind your back. They will mostly not say these things to your face. Some of the signs that your reputation has been attacked are that you are left out of social activities and people seem overly eager to see the worst in you.

Teen: How do I build a good reputation?

You: This is fairly simple. Treat other people well and keep your word. If you say you're going to do something, do it. Don't make promises you're not going to keep. Be the person you say you are.

Teen: How do I protect my reputation?

You: This is harder to do in the world of social media than ever before. Some guidelines:

- Use the nana rule – don't post anything online that you wouldn't want your nana to see.

- Beware of job-stoppers – these are pictures or comments that a future employer could use to not employ you and includes photos of being trashed at parties, doing anything illegal, groping people or promoting drugs, racism, sexism or violence.

- Don't post negative comments about anyone.

- Have two Facebook profiles – a private one for friends and a public one for everyone else.

- Your private profile should have maximum privacy settings.

- Set a Google alert for your name. Google will send you an email if your name is posted anywhere online.

- If you want to make comments on chat rooms or blogs, don't use your full name.

- If you see something that upsets you, and you feel compelled to respond, wait 24 hours before replying.

- If you post comments about other people, never write when you're angry.

Essential conversation 9 – How to take care of yourself

Life is full of great moments but it also has setbacks and obstacles. Knowing how to endure difficult times and rise above them is essential. Here are a few tips to pass onto your teens.

Keep in touch with your friends   Friends and family are your greatest treasures. Keep in touch with them. A quick message on social media or a catch up over coffee can be enough. Don't be drawn into a silly game of thinking they should contact you first. Be the person to initiate a catch up. That way you end up with more friends – and deeper friendships.

You are responsible for what you put into your body and what comes out   What you eat and drink or smoke has an effect on you. It sometimes seem that many people around the world gobble down junk food and sugary drinks without much conscious thought that this might have some consequence for their well-being. The same applies to sex. If you place bodily fluids into someone else or have them placed into you be aware there can be consequences.

Make playlists to help in tough times   Music powerfully accesses our emotions. Create two playlists of songs. One for times when you feel hurt, sad and bruised by life. It's good to have some music to help you express these feelings and at the same time, realise that you're not the only person to have felt this way. The second playlist is upbeat and is selected to help you return to a happy, more powerful and pumped state of mind.

Make to-do lists   A lot of people waste a lot of time because they don't plan. They just wait till life shows up. To stand apart, make a to-do list. Write down the things you need to get done. Give each a priority order. Ask yourself, if I got nothing else done today, which of these would be the most essential? That gets an A rating, the next a B and so on. Consider developing this so you have weekly plans and even yearly ones. If you find yourself having trouble sleeping, get into the practice of making a to-do list for tomorrow last thing before you go to bed.

> Life works well when you have time for spontaneous fun.

Keep track of your achievements   Keep your to-lists in a diary or book and tick them off as you accomplish them.

Develop routines and mini habits   Life works well when you have time for spontaneous fun. To have those times freed up, you may also need routines and habits. Developing and scheduling times to have health checks and dental reviews sounds tedious until you think of the pain that not having them can cause.

People often start each year with grand plans about getting fit, losing weight and being more successful. Big shifts in your habits are hard to maintain. Instead, develop a mini habit. Instead of planning to go to the gym three times a week for thirty minutes each time, start by doing one push up. Instead of going on a drastic diet, give yourself a fifteen-minute delay. So if a cream bun or the smell of donuts comes into your awareness, think to yourself, 'I'll wait fifteen minutes. If I still want it them, I'll decide then.'

Some examples of mini habits:

1 Say hello to one person each day that you don't know.

2 Give two people a compliment each day.

3 Climb some stairs each day.

4 Listen to a favourite song and relax to it.

5 Think three positive thoughts.

6 Forgive someone for something.

7 Message at least one friend.

8 Read two pages of a book.

9 Go outside and walk 40 paces.

10 Drink one glass of water.

Daily gratitude Make a daily practice of counting your assets. Notice the people we feel thankful towards and the events that go well helps us to be happier.

Limit media consumption Your brain can only process so much information. When you need to be focused on schoolwork, don't overtax your brain with social media, computer games, videos or television.

Do the tough stuff first If you hold the tasks you don't like doing until later, you will often not get around to doing them. But your mind won't let you forget it! You will keep thinking about what you have to do. As a result, you will spend a lot more time thinking about and avoiding the task than you need. It is better to get it over and done with and then get on with having a happy time.

Essential conversation 10 – How to be an adult

The entire purpose of this book has been to help you guide your teen into the world of independent, self-reliant, early adulthood. Many of the ructions and frictions you may have experienced as your teen develops have been about finding a way to steer their own lives.

The whole point of adolescence is that it is a stepping stone on the way to becoming an independent adult. Even when young people enter their twenties, this process is incomplete.

When we start any new phase of life, we need support. Your fledgling young adult will need your support, love and care. This is adulthood with learner plates on.

The conversations that will help them to become an adult are the ones that will occur over years. Some of the topics that are commonly covered are outlined below.

Money and jobs

Unless you are contemplating providing your teen with financial care for the rest of their lives, they will need to find some way of finding their own cash. There are seven ways to acquire money:

1   Create something you can sell to someone else.

2   Get a job.

3   Inherit it.

4   Obtain a gift.

5   Marry someone with money.

6   Go on welfare.

7   Steal.

Let's rule out a few of these possibilities early on:

Inherit it   Don't count on it.

Steal it   Risk of long jail sentences.

Obtain a gift   Good luck!

Go on welfare   Not a pathway towards a happy life.

That leaves three other ways.

Marry someone with money   If you're lucky enough to fall in love with someone who is rich or makes a lot of money, that's great. Being with someone *only* because they have money won't make you happy. It will make you miserable.

Sell something you create   Making something you can sell to someone else can bring in funds, but it also is a hit and miss affair. Starting a business can be a great way to obtain money, but it can also take a few false starts before you succeed. Don't be disheartened. Have a motto, 'There is no such thing as failure, there is only feedback.' Selling your artworks, crafts, books, music or creations at fairs and markets or on Ebay may be a way to attain financial security. However, it may take you quite a while to latch onto the right recipe to be in demand.

Get a job   For most people, the path towards independence begins with employment. Even people who end up running businesses often learn their trade while employed by someone else.

Getting jobs

Most likely, you will need to prepare a resume. Have a look online for tips on writing great resumes that stand out. The next step is the interview. A job interview is like a first date. It's a bit scary for both sides. Both people are trying to work out if the match between the two of them is going to work. If the interview works out well, it is the start of a relationship.

> A job interview is like a first date.

A couple of key tips for succeeding at job interviews:

- Dress as if you were already working in that field.

- Be neat and clean.

- Employers are more interested about hearing what you can do for them than they are about hearing about what they can do for you.

- Prepare. Know the details of the position, the duties and the main features of the organisation.

- Be likeable and enthusiastic – employers want to be around people they like and who are upbeat about their role.

- Listen to the interviewer. Don't interrupt. Don't avoid their questions and don't waste their time with long rambling answers.

- Give the employer one or two notable ways to remember you. It could be an interest you share in common or it could be that you outline how you will contribute as soon as you star the job. If you bring a specific skill, show how it could be used to help out.

- Don't complain about your current employer, your past co-workers, or customers. Stay upbeat and positive.

- Be yourself. Don't lie or misrepresent yourself. If you're asked about your biggest weakness, don't reply with the hammy, overused, 'I'm a perfectionist.' Instead say, 'It changes. I seek out feedback from people I work with about my shortcomings and address them as soon as I can.'

> Listen to the interviewer. Don't interrupt.

- At the end of the interview, ask as many questions as you need to, to determine if the job is for you.

If you decide that you would like the job, let the employer know. Tell them you think you are the right person for the job and why. You could say something like, 'This job is a great fit for me. I can bring you skills in people management, which is exactly what I am looking to do more of.'

You could then ask something like, 'Is there anything else I can tell you to help you decide that I'm the right person for this job?' If you feel it is appropriate, you could follow up the interview with a brief thank you note or email.

Keeping jobs

Here are a couple of tips to keeping a job.

- Do your best. Very few people do their best. If you do, it will set you apart.

- Be on time. Being late conveys rudeness and a lack of caring.

- If you know you can't avoid being late or absent, call in.

- Know that employers notice if you take sick days off on Mondays or Fridays, days before or after public holidays and your birthday.

- Be keen and enthusiastic. Look for opportunities to be helpful.

- Never complain about your boss, your team or your customers. Anywhere. Not to other employees and certainly not on social media.

- Aim to develop positive working relationships with everyone.

- Think long and hard before you start a romantic relationship with a work colleague.

- Never say to your boss, 'That's not my job.'

- Request feedback from your boss about how to improve. Once you've received some feedback ask, 'Would it be OK to check in with you again in a few weeks to review how it's going?' You want to be seen as responsive to feedback, but not overly dependent on supervision.

Essential conversation 11 – How to manage living independently

The fine art of living independently could take up a whole book. However, the key to it is budgeting. Charles Dickens summed it up in *David Copperfield*: 'Annual income twenty pounds, annual expenditure nineteen six, result happiness. Annual income twenty pounds, annual expenditure twenty pounds ought and six, result misery.' Find a good budgeting tool and help your young adult to work their way through it. Most of the items on the list will be things they have not considered.

Laundry   Some teens live in a fanciful world with a magical laundry where dirty clothes enter and reappear washed and ironed and ready for use. Sadly, independent living requires that the laundry myth go the same way as Santa Claus, the Easter Bunny and the Tooth Fairy. All things must pass.

'What do I do now all my shirts are pink?'

After a few attempts by your independently living young adult to show up around dinnertime with a bag of washing, the time has come to introduce your young adult, if you haven't done so beforehand, to the dark arts of the laundry. A few early disasters can be expected. You can expect a few emergency calls, 'What do I do now all my shirts are pink?' Some items will shrink; others will stretch to gargantuan proportions. This phase is called 'learning'.

Essential conversation 12 – Finding romance

Romance appears in life in the most unexpected times and places.

- Be yourself. Go out.

- Become a good conversationalist. Ask people about themselves. Don't focus too much on whether this person will be the one you end up with. Instead, focus on having a good chat. If it is right, conversation will flow.

> Become a good conversationalist. Ask people about themselves.

- Be scrupulously clean. Smell good to be close to.

- Meet lots of people. You need to let enough people catch your eye so that some of them can catch your heart.

Saying no to romance you don't want Everyone gets a bit scared at times that they won't find the right person. Even if you're lonely, don't say yes to people you don't want to be with. Firstly, it's not fair on them to lead them on and later disappoint them. Secondly, it's not fair on you. The stress caused by starting something and then having misgivings is enormous.

Keeping romances It's likely that not all of your romances will continue. Some will die a natural death as you learn that you are not as suited as first appeared to be the case. This realisation can be hard to cope with. It is useful to consider that some relationships are just not meant to be.

Once you do find someone you really want to be with, love him or her passionately, wholeheartedly and openly and also remember to keep growing and developing yourself. Maintain contact with your friends. Don't drop your interests or life passions just because you've found someone. Consider your partner's needs and interests and also be attentive to your own. Successful relationships are not just about finding the right person, but about being the right person.

And remember ...

Conversations matter, but not as much as your actions. The way you live is the model most tricky teens will use as a model for their lives. If you live a life of envy, bitterness and distance, they will emulate you. Live an openhearted life of generosity and fun and they will follow that path.

Most tricky teens end up functioning well as adults. They do get jobs, find partners, buy homes and look after themselves. The big issue is whether they live happy and fulfilling lives. Here's where you come in. The example that you set them will determine that. If you want your tricky teen to have a great life, the place to begin is on creating a great life for yourself.

Acknowledgements

I am lucky enough to have a fantastic publishing and production team and I'd like to express my deep appreciation for the creative genius and support of Rex Finch, Samantha Miles and Laura Boon.

I am also blessed to have around me a wonderful group of people who inspire me and veer me away from some of my wilder and erratic ideas. These people include:

Anthony and Di Beardall, Bob Bellhouse, Cheryl and Brian Critchley, Noel Cranswick, Lorraine Day, Paul Dillon, Mary Duma, Rod Dungan, Vicki, Sam and Lucy Fuller, Vicki Hartley, Mark Holland, Neil and Jane Hawkes, John Hendry, Brenda Hosking-Brown, Terry Janz, Nell Jones, Ola Krupinska, Ian Larsen, Karen McGraw, Catie McNamara, Robert McNeilly, Chris Mackie, Cindy Mathers, Carolyn Meir, Michael Nagel, Georgie Nutton, Ramech Manocha, Peter O'Connor, Ric Pawsey, Robert Schweitzer, Michael Schwarz, Bob Sharples, Liz and Trevor Sheahan, Michele Silva, Helen Street, Stan Tatkin, David Tyson, Bert Van Halen, Andrew Wicking, Peter Wicking, Peter Wiltshire and Paul Wood.

Author notes

Welcome to the war of independence

Page 10 'As Daniel Segiel says ... ' Siegel, D.J. (2013) *Brainstorm – The Power and Purpose of the Teenage Brain*, Penguin, New York.

Page 11 'While all tricky teens are unique...' The idea of life trajectories has been developed by many researchers. This approach was discussed elegantly by Bruce Compas and I have enlarged upon his ideas in my own research. Compas, B. (1995), 'Adolescent Development: Pathways of Risk and Resilience', *Annual Review of Psychology*, 46, 265–93.

Page 13 '...the world of tricky teens has got younger.' Spear, L.P. (2000) 'The adolescent brain and age-related behavioral manifestations', *Neuroscience and Biobehavioral Reviews*, 24, 417–463. Spear, L.P. (2000) 'Neurobehavioral changes in adolescence', *Current Directions in Psychological Science*, 9, 4, 111–114.

Page 14 'It increases between ten and twenty times ....' Brizendine, L. (2006) *The Female Brain*, Bantam, New York.

Page 14 'Boys have a twenty-fold increase ...' Brizendine, L. (2010) *The Male Brain*, Broadway Books, New York.

Page 15 'The research indicates that this almost always not true.' Moffit, T.E. (1993), 'Adolescence limited and life course persistent antisocial behaviour: A developmental taxonomy', *Psychological Review*, 100, 674–701.Fergusson, D.M. and Lynsky, M.T. (1996) 'Adolescent resiliency to family adversity', *Journal of Child Psychology and Psychiatry and Allied Disciplines*, 37, 3, 281–292.

Page 18 'In the early 1990s ...' Fuller, A., McGraw, K. and Goodyear, M. (2002) 'Bungy-Jumping Through Life: A developmental framework for the promotion of resilience', In L. Rowling, G. Martin & L. Walker, (eds.) *Mental Health and Young People*, Sydney, McGraw-Hill.

Giedd, J.N., Snell, J.W., Lange, J.C. Rajapakse, B.J.. Casey, B.J., Kozuch, P.L., Vaituzis, A.C., Vauss, Y.C., Hamburger, S.D., Kaysen, D. and Rapoport, J.L. (1996) Quantitative magnetic resonance imaging of human brain development: ages 4 to 18, *Cerebral Cortex*, 6, 551–560.

Peper, J.S. and Dahl, R. E. (2013) 'The Teenage Brain: Surging hormones – brain-behavior interactions during puberty', *Current Directions in Psychological Science* 2013 22: 134.

Neurochemistry and habit

Page 27 'Pieter Rossouw describes ...' The Neuroscience of Anxiety workshop, attended Aug 13, 2013.

The rest of this chapter is drawn from a composite of sources, including:

Bunsey, M and Eichenbaum, H. (1996) 'Conservation of hippocampal memory function in rats and humans', *Nature*, 379, 255–257.

Fiorillo, C.D., Tobler, P.N. and Schultz, W. (2003) 'Discrete coding of reward probability and uncertainty by dopamine neurons', *Science*, 299, 1898–1902.

Gazzaniga, M.S. (2004) *The Cognitive Neurosciences 111*, London, MIT Press.

Giedd, J.N., Snell, J.W., Lange, J.C. Rajapakse, B.J.. Casey, B.J., Kozuch, P.L., Vaituzis, A.C., Vauss, Y.C., Hamburger, S.D., Kaysen, D. and Rapoport, J.L. (1996) Quantitative magnetic resonance imaging of human brain development: ages 4 to 18, *Cerebral Cortex*, 6, 551–560.

Anxiety and worry busting

This chapter is drawn from a composite of sources, including:

Gould, E. (2004) 'Stress, Deprivation and Adult Neurogenesis' in M. Gazzaniga (ed.) *The Cognitive Neurosciences*. Schultz, J.M. (2002) 'Getting Formal with Dopamine and Reward, *Neuron*, 36, 241–263.

Schultz, J.M., Dayan, P. and Montague, P.R. (1997) 'A Neural Substrate of Prediction and Reward', *Science*, 275, 1593–1599.

Spear, L.P. (2010) *The Behavioral Neuroscience of Adolescence*, W.W. Norton: New York. Spear, L.P. (2000) 'The Adolescent Brain and Age-related Behavioral Manifestations', *Neuroscience and Biobehavioral Reviews*, 24, 417–463.

Spear, L.P. (2000) 'Neurobehavioral Changes in Adolescence', *Current Directions in Psychological Science*, 9, 4, 111–114.

Page 33 **'Charles Duhigg in his wonderful book ...'** Duhigg, C. (2012) *The Power of Habit: Why we do what we do in life and business*, Random House, New York.

Page 40 **'Oliver Emberton cleverly describes ...** 'Emberton, O. <www.quora.com/Procrastination/How-do-I-get-over-my-bad-habit-of-procrastinating/answer/Oliver-Emberton> (downloaded 23 March 2014).

Page 44 **'... Jane McGonigal's TED talk ...'** McGonigal, J. TED talk <www.youtube.com/watch?v=lfBpsV1Hwqs> (downloaded 23 March 2014).

Page 45 **'A Taiwanese study compared students ...'** Bronson, P and Merryman, A. (2013) Why can some kids handle pressure while others fall apart? *The New York Times* <www.nytimes.com/2013/02/10/magazine/why-can-some-kids-handle-pressure-while-others-fall-apart.html?_r=0> (downloaded 23 March 2014).

Colvin, G. (2008). *Talent is Overrated: What really separates world class performers from everybody else*, Nicholas Brealey Publishing, London.

Romeo, R.D. (2013). 'The Teenage Brain: The stress response and the adolescent brain' *Current Directions in Psychological Science* 2013 22: 140

Page 46 ' **A study conducted by Jeremy Jamieson at the University of Rochester ...**' Jamieson, J.P., Mendes, W. B. and Nock, M. K. (2013) 'Improving Acute Stress

Responses, The Power of Reappraisal', *Current Directions in Psychological Science*, 22, 51-56.

Belonging and attachment

Page 59 'About half of us won the lottery of life.' Wallin, D.J. (2007) *Attachment in Psychotherapy*, Guilford Press, New York.

Tatkin, S. (2013) *PACT Psychobiological Approaches to Couple Therapy*, address Melbourne November 2013.

Boy smarts

This chapter is drawn from a composite of sources, including:

Gurian, M. (2001) *Boys and Girls Learn Differently!* Jossey-Bass, San Francisco.

Hawkes, T. (2001) *Boy oh Boy – How to Educate and Raise Boys*, Prentice Hall, Sydney.

James, A.N. (2007) *Teaching the Male Brain: how boys think, feel and learn in school*, Corwin, California.

Zimbardo, P. (2012) *The Demise of Guys*, TED Books.

Communication

This chapter is drawn from a composite of sources, including:

Deida, D. (2004) *The Way of the Superior Man*, Sounds True, Boulder.

Shafir, R.Z. (2000) *The Zen of Listening*, Quest, Wheaton.

Tannen, D. (1990) *You Just Don't Understand Me*, Random, Sydney.

Tannen, D. (2006) *You're Wearing That? Understanding mothers and daughters in conversation*, Ballantine, New York.

Zeldin, T. (1998) *Conversation: How talk can change our lives*, Hidden Spring, Mahwah.

Page 89 'Skilled hypnotherapist Milton Erickson ...' Haley, J. (1973) *Uncommon Therapy: The psychiatric techniques of Milton Erickson*, New York, Norton.

Computer addiction

Page 93 'By the age of 21, teens will have spent ...' Thomas, D. and Seely Brown, J. (2011) *A New Culture of Learning: Cultivating the imagination for a world of constant change.*

Page 93 'The differences between teens and their parents ...' Thomas, D. and Seely Brown, J. (2011) *A New Culture of Learning: Cultivating the imagination for a world of constant change.*

Page 97 ' Nicholas Carr calls this shift "mind flit" ...' Carr, N. (2011) *The Shallows* W.W. Norton and Co, New York.

Page 98 'Teens are more intelligent than ever before... in 1950.' Keating, D.P. (1990) 'Adolescent Thinking' in Feldman, S.S. and Elliot, G.R. (Eds.) *At the Threshold: The developing adolescent*, Cambridge, MA, Harvard University Press. (pp. 54–89).

Page 99 '**Also, the increase in awkwardness and shyness...**' Zimbardo, P. (2012) *The Demise of Guys*, TED Books.

Carrington, V. (2005) 'Txting: the end of civilization (again)?' *Cambridge Journal of Education*, 35, 2, 161–175.

Gee, J.P. (2003) *What Video Games Have to Teach Us About Learning and Literacy*, Palgarve: London.

Page 102 '**For example, if you want to block your teen's laptop ...**' An example can be found at <www.ianswerguy.com/limit-internet-access-using-router-settings/> (downloaded 23 March 2014).

Confidence

Page 108 '**This is known as deliberate practice...**' Colvin Clark, R. (2008) *Building Expertise – Cognitive Methods for Training and Performance Improvement* Pfieffer, New York.

Depression

Page 112 '**Leafy greens have magnesium ...**' Ross, J. (2002) *The Mood Cure*, Thorsons, London.

Page 112 '**We experience flow ...**' Csikszentmihalyi, M (1990) *Flow: The psychology of happiness*, Rider Press, London.

Page 115 '**Moderate exercise for ten minutes a day ...**' Amen, D. (2005) *Making a Good Brain Great*, Harmony Books:,New York and Yapko, M.D. (1997) *Breaking the patterns of depression*, Broadway Books, New York.

Page 116 '**Learn these and teach them to your teen ...**' Cohen, A. (2005) *Why your life sucks and what you can do about it*, Bantam Books, New York.

Drugs and alcohol

Page 120 '**Figures vary from county to county ...**' National Drug Strategy documents see http://www.nationaldrugstrategy.gov.au/internet/drugstrategy/Publishing.nsf/content/2C4E3D846787E47BCA2577E600173CBE/$File/sch4.pdf.

Page 123 '**By the time most adults are ready for a good lie down ...**' Spear, L. (2013) 'The Teenage Brain: Adolescents and alcohol', *Current Directions in Psychological Science*, 22: 152.

Page 125 '**Ten quick reasons why teens should not use alcohol.**' I am grateful to have had conversations with specialists in this area including John Tomborou, Michael Nagel, Paul Dillon and Bob Bellhouse.

Girl smarts

This chapter is drawn from a composite of sources, including:

Brizendine, L. (2006) *The Female Brain*, Bantam, New York.

Gurian, M. (2001) *Boys and Girls Learn Differently!* Jossey-Bass, San Francisco.

James, A.N. (2009) *Teaching the Female Brain: How girls learn math and science,* Corwin, California.

Ideal day

This chapter is drawn from a composite of sources, including:

Benton, D. and Owens, D.S. (1993) Blood glucose and human memory. *Psychopharmacology,* 113, 83–88.

Benton, D and Sargent, J. (1992) Breakfast, blood glucose and memory, *Biological Psychology,* 33, 595–607.

Foster, R. and Krieitzman, L. (2004) *Rhythms of Life: The biological clocks that control the daily lives of every living thing,* Profile Books, London.

Mednick, S., Nakayama, K. and Stickgold, R. (2003) Sleep dependent learning: a nap is a good as a night. *Nature Neuroscience,* 6, 7, 697–698.

Ross, J. (2002) *The Mood Cure* Thorsons, London.

Siegel, J. (2001) The REM Sleep–memory Consolidation Hypothesis, *Science,* 274, 2 November, 1058–1063.

Motivation

This chapter is drawn from a composite of sources, including:

Csikszentmihalyi, M (1990) *Flow: The psychology of happiness,* Rider Press, London.

Loehr, J and Schwartz (2005) *The Power of Full Engagement,* Free Press, New York.

Martin, A (2010) Building Classroom Success Eliminating Academic Fear and Failure, conference presentation.

Rathvon, N. (1996) *The Unmotivated Child – Helping your underachiever become a successful student,* New York, Simon and Schuster.

Luna, B., Paulsen, D.J., Padmanabhan, A. and Geier, C. (2013) The Teenage Brain: Cognitive Control and Motivation, *Current Directions in Psychological Science* 22: 94.

Perfectionism

Page 150 'High achievers also want great outcomes ...' Belliok, S. (2011) *Choke,* Melbourne University Press, Carlton.

Page 153 'Timothy Gallwey wrote a series of books ...' Gallwey, W.T. (1975). *The Inner Game of Tennis* Pan, Chatam, Kent.

Pessimism

Page 157 'There were 5126 failures...' http://www.rd.com/advice/work-career/james-dyson-on-creating-a-vacuum-that-actually-well-sucks/

Dweck, C. (1984). The power of negative thinking, *Times Educational Supplement,* London, 21 September.

Sexuality and romance

This chapter is drawn from a composite of sources, including:

Page 175 'Gordon Livingston, in his wonderful book ...' Livingston. G. (2009) *How to Love: Who best to love and how best to love,* Hachette, Sydney.

Page 175 'Robin Skynner and John Cleese ...' Cleese, J. Skynner, R. (1983) *Families and How to Survive Them,* Methueon, London.

Livingstone, G. (2005) *Too Soon Old, Too late Smart – Thirty things you need to know now,* Hodder, Sydney.

Siblings

Page 185 'In a survey of over 250 000 parents ...' This survey has been conducted with the 250 000 parents who have attended my parenting seminars.

Suicide

Page 186 'In one study by Dr Karen McGraw, 19 per cent ...' McGraw, K. (2005). *The Role of Connectedness in the Transition from Secondary School to Tertiary Education: A longitudinal study.* Professional Doctorate of Psychology. Swinburne University, Australia.

Twentysomethings

This chapter is drawn from a composite of sources, including:

Friday, N. (1982) *My Mother Myself,* Fontana/Collins, Glasgow.

Levine, M. (2005) *Ready or Not, Here Life Comes,* New York, Simon and Schuster.

Know them better than they know themselves

Page 207 'Garry Chapman, in his book ...' Chapman, G.(2000) *The Five Love Languages of Teenagers,* Northfiled Publishing, Chicago.

Week two of The Six-Week Plan

Page 227 'As Russ Harris so cleverly points out...' Harris, R. (2010) *The Confidence Gap: From fear to freedom,* Constable and Robinson, London.

Essential conversations

Page 282 'Develop routines and mini habits' Guise, S. How Simple Mini Habits Can Change Your Life' <http://tinybuddha.com/blog/simple-mini-habits-can-change-life> (downloaded 23 March 2014).

Page 284 'There are seven ways to acquire money.' Toffler, A. and Toffler, H (2006) *Revolutionary Wealth,* Knopf, New York.